SHAPES OF THE CHURCH TO COME

To the people and clergy of the
Diocese of Rochester

Shapes of the Church to Come

MICHAEL NAZIR-ALI

KINGSWAY PUBLICATIONS
EASTBOURNE

Copyright © Michael Nazir-Ali 2001

The right of Michael Nazir-Ali to be identified
as the author of this work has been asserted by him in
accordance with the Copyright, Designs
and Patents Act 1988.

First published 2001

All rights reserved.
No part of this publication may be reproduced or
transmitted in any form or by any means, electronic
or mechanical, including photocopy, recording or any
information storage and retrieval system, without
permission in writing from the publisher.

Unless otherwise indicated, biblical quotations are
from the New International Version © 1973, 1978, 1984
by the International Bible Society.
RSV=Revised Standard Version © 1946, 1952, 1971,
1973 by the Division of Christian Education of the National
Council of the Churches of Christ in the USA.

Some names have been changed to protect identities.

ISBN 0 85476 891 2

Published by
KINGSWAY COMMUNICATIONS LTD
Lottbridge Drove, Eastbourne, BN23 6NT, England.
Email: books@kingsway.co.uk

Book design and production for the publishers by
Bookprint Creative Services, P.O. Box 827, BN21 3YJ, England.
Printed in Great Britain.

Contents

Foreword

In *The Church Looks Forward*, published just a few months before his death and as the maelstrom of the Second World War continued to rage, Archbishop William Temple sought to discern how the church might best respond to the climactic changes which that war had unleashed upon society. Now, nearly 60 years on and in a world of ever-accelerating change which Temple himself would scarcely even begin to recognise, Bishop Michael Nazir-Ali addresses those same daunting yet compelling questions: what should the church in the twenty-first century be *like*, and what should it be *doing*?

That there should be deep resonances between their two perspectives will come as no surprise. In the Divine Economy, the relationship between creator and created admits of no essential change: and it is with the same destructive forces of alienation that the church must always contend. Both men confront the reality of this latter evil. Temple speaks of the headlong individualism which leads to chaos; Nazir-Ali of the naïve credulity and world-weary cynicism which erodes capacity for engagement with the absolute. For both, however, the church's future can only lie in a courageous openness: in *encounter.* It is the sort of encounter that the Archbishop described in terms of 'loyalty and adventure', and that Bishop Michael sees as the way in which the resources of Tradition and Scripture combine to guide and empower us as we set out to discover new ways of 'being church' in the twenty-first century.

In his consideration of the *shapes* of tomorrow's church (note, not *shape*), he recognises the inevitability and the propriety of a degree of diversity and plurality in the global ecclesiastical market place. In this Bishop Nazir-Ali reflects a number of my own concerns expressed in the sermon I preached before the University of Cambridge and to which he makes reference in this book.

The Bishop brings many gifts to his task. Not least among them the sort of life experience that enables him to assess the many cross-cultural currents which shape contemporary thinking, as well as an undoubted depth of scholarship and (every bit as important!) the ability to make that scholarship accessible to his reader.

He presents a view that is at once upbeat yet fully cognizant of the church's situation. From church plants to the Establishment, his examination is searching and his diagnosis compelling. However, although he does suggest ways in which we might move forward, he is also wise enough to know that the church to come is not a matter in which bishops or archbishops can be prescriptive. It is the *whole* church, at every level, that – under God – must share in shaping its future. Bishop

Nazir-Ali's contribution to equipping us for this task is as timely as it is important.

Dr David Hope
Archbishop of York

An Introductory Word

This book is about what the church is to be and the jobs it has to do in a quickly changing world and in cultures that delight in being 'postmodern' and 'post-Christian'. As a bishop I am, of course, a practitioner, and have written from that point of view. This book is an attempt to equip Christians with resources to live and witness effectively in a world such as ours. This does involve investigation of what the Bible has to say and how Christians have responded to their situation in other ages and cultures, but these are always related to actual opportunities and problems facing us today.

The stories here are supposed to alert us to the issues we need to address, and to do this we need to go to the Bible and the developing thought and practice of the church, as well as to other disciplines. The church is concerned with specific (and sometimes quite small) local communities, but also, on a larger scale, with government plans for urban or rural regeneration and the implications for pastoral care and mission of these plans. Both ends of our concern receive attention here.

Much of what we face is new and unfamiliar. This can have the effect of making us withdraw into our own shells and refuse to relate to what is around us. I hope that this book will give Christians confidence in the biblical and spiritual resources available to us as we seek to witness today.

Finally, I have tried to write about controversial matters that have divided Christians in the past, in such a way as to transcend past divisions and to approach the issues with fresh eyes and an open mind, relying on recent scholarship to do this. The aim is always to build up the *unity in truth* of all Christians, regardless of their denominational allegiance.

I pray that God will use this little effort to renew the church and make it an effective instrument of the divine mission.

1. Is There a Gospel for the Twenty-First Century?

CASE STUDY

Zoë is up at 6 a.m.: she is a single mother now (her 'partner' disappeared long ago) and she has to get the children off to school single-handed. In between the cereals and toast, as well as repeatedly hurrying the children on, she manages a glance at the papers. She is a chartered secretary, so looks first at the business section, but then, a little guiltily, at the horoscope. Do the stars hold out any hope for her? Soon it is time to go. As she plunges into her busy world of children, school, office and colleagues, there is no more time for reflection. It is only at night when she goes to bed that there is time again to wonder . . .

What is good news for Zoë? Is there a gospel for the age in which we live? If so, how can it be communicated and what sort of church do we need if we are going to be effective in this task?

For every age and clime

The questions can only be answered by first recognising that the mission of the Christian church has been universal from the very beginning. The seeds of such a universality are deeply embedded in the testimony of the Older Testament, that God has a saving purpose for the whole world and that the nation of Israel has been chosen to be a vehicle (but not the only one) in the fulfilment of God's purposes. The mission of Jesus, likewise, was deliberately exercised in the plural environment around the Sea of Galilee and beyond. The Gospels, as well as recent archaeological discoveries, confirm that Jesus had extensive contact with Gentiles during his public ministry.[1]

When the church's mission arrived on the world stage with explosive force, its roots were still in the ministry and mission of Jesus and in a particular understanding of the first Christians' Bible (our Old Testament). The early date of some of St Paul's letters (e.g. Galatians, written as early as AD 48 or 49) and of the Council of Jerusalem (Acts 15:6–29) show us how quickly the church came to understand its worldwide task.

Many account for the speed with which the good news of Jesus Christ spread in terms of the relative unity of the Roman Empire, the stability it provided through the enforcement of the *Pax Romana* and the development of a common culture and language throughout the Mediterranean world.[2] There is, of course, much truth in these accounts, but we must not underestimate the great diversity there was *within* the Roman Empire, nor can we ignore the fact that the gospel spread far beyond its borders: to Ethiopia, Armenia and the Persian Empire (to give a few examples). In the first few centuries the church was established in all three continents of the ancient world: Asia, Africa and Europe. One of the reasons for the rapid spread of the Christian faith has to do with what has been called the 'translatability' of the gospel into the worldview, the thought forms, the idiom and the values of the different cultures into which it arrives. This is not only the rendering of the Scriptures into the language of a particular ethnic or cultural group (though that is important, of course). It is, rather, the assimilation of gospel truth into a community. This can have quite unexpected results for those who have transmitted the faith, as well as for those who have received it. The spontaneity and exuberance as well as the deep spirituality and commitment to human wholeness, which are so characteristic of the best of African Christianity, reveal how interaction with the gospel has highlighted and strengthened God-given aspects of African cultures.[3]

It is true, of course, that the gospel can also challenge existing customs and ways of thinking or living. Archbishop David Gitari of Kenya, in an important address to the 1988 Lambeth Conference of Anglican bishops, distinguished between what the gospel cannot tolerate (he cited infanticide, cattle-rustling and witchcraft as examples from his own culture), what it can tolerate for the time being (such as polygamy for the first generation of converts) and what it endorses and transforms (such as an understanding of our humanity in terms of community).[4]

In a remarkable speech to the Roman Catholic bishops of Asia, Cardinal Joseph Ratzinger of the Vatican drew attention to the power of the Christian faith both to create culture and to interact with cultures so as to bring about a mutual deepening and transformation: cultures are changed by the gospel but the gospel also is expressed in fresh ways.[5] It is not only that the universal church exhibits certain cultural features and values. This is so because of the demands of the Christian faith, but the gospel can also bring about a transformation in cultures that is nothing less than the emergence of new cultures. There are several examples of this happening throughout the course of history. The culture of the Armenians is often referred to as one that has almost wholly been created by Christian influence. The conversion of King Tiridates by St Gregory the Illuminator, the invention of the alphabet by St Mesrob so that the Scriptures, Liturgy and other Christian literature could be translated, and the organisation of church and nation by Nerses the Great, all provided the impetus for the development of Armenian art, literature and social organisation.

What is true of Armenia is true also of Ethiopia. Here also the structures of state and of popular culture were Christianised very early, and coherence was provided by the translation of the Scriptures and early Christian writings into *Ge'ez*, the ancient language of Ethiopia. Although it was mainly the monks who engaged in mission among the non-Christians, they often had popular and even state support.[6]

The work of Saints Cyril and Methodius among the Slav people is another example of the faith's translatability and its capacity to create a civilisation and a culture that is at the same time distinctive and Christian. For their part Sanneh and other African theologians are aware of the importance of the encounter, challenge and assimilation taking place today in Africa as distinctively Christian cultures emerge on that continent. None of this is to say that these cultures are perfect or that the gospel has not been distorted in them during the course of history – only that they have been influenced and moulded by Christian faith and values.

In his ground-breaking work on the history of Christianisation in Europe, Professor Anton Wessels has analysed the extent to which the process involved genuine encounter and transformation. He goes on then to explore the significance of history for the evangelisation of contemporary Europe.[7] The gospel is not, of course, a disembodied message that can be hawked from culture to culture. It is incarnate in people's lifestyle, relationships and values. It is this 'embodied' faith that encounters and transforms cultures, while, at the same time, remaining dynamic itself; this inherent translatability makes the mission of the church universal. In the twenty-first century we have to ask how the encounter is to take place and how the gospel is to make sense in contemporary culture.

The big story

Another reason for the spread of the Christian faith is that the gospel is a 'big story'. That is, it claims to give an account of every aspect of life: our own existence, that of the universe, why we are here, our purpose and destiny. From the very beginning there have, of course, been other 'big stories'. The mystery religions of the ancient world were big stories and the Christian story had to compete with them. Neoplatonism is a philosophical system with religious overtones. It was another big story and a formidable opponent of early Christianity. There was a complex mixture of conflict, dialogue and assimilation in relation to these big stories, but the fact remains that they were replaced by Christianity in the Roman Empire, at least. The triumph in the Persian Empire was much more partial.[8]

If there is to be genuine encounter between the gospel and contemporary cultures, we have to ask, 'What are today's big stories?' Many different answers can be given to such a question, but let us examine just three of today's big stories that are relevant to evangelisation.

The first big story is, in fact, a number of stories: these are the stories told by the other living religions of the world. They are, of course, dissimilar from one another and, to a greater or lesser degree, different from the Christian faith. In our day we are learning to co-operate with these other faiths and are relating to them through dialogue, witness and service. We are acknowledging the need to listen to one another and to learn from each other. In certain areas, such as common values for the community and the struggle for justice and compassion in society, it is possible, indeed desirable, to co-operate with people of other faiths.

Nevertheless, there cannot be complementarity in its fullest sense. When all is said and done, the gospel, and therefore Christian mission, must make a claim to distinctiveness in its analysis of the human situation and the remedy needed for its ills. Many other religions make a similar claim. This creates the need and the context for *choice*. Whatever the co-operation, however deep the dialogue and the friendship, there will always be a moment of crisis when people must choose between the Christian faith and another faith. One of the most important tasks today for the international community, as well as for nation-states, is to make sure that individuals and communities can, indeed, exercise their right to choose the system of belief and values by which they are to live and die.

The second of today's big stories is what we might call *post-Enlightenment modernism* – a long term, but let me hasten to explain what I mean. At the time of the so-called Enlightenment in the seventeenth and eighteenth centuries, religion was separated from the processes of observation, deliberation and reflection, which were held to be scientific and rational, while religion was seen as being about feeling, emotion and values. It was, moreover, assigned a place in the private sphere of human life, and was denied a role in the public sphere of policy-making.[9] Although the Enlightenment led to notable achievements in the areas of personal liberty and of welfare provision, its attitude to religion led to a largely materialistic view of the human condition that could not, adequately, account for other Enlightenment values, such as the inalienable dignity of all human beings. Religion, in the meantime, which could have provided the means for grounding and spreading some of the Enlightenment's more beneficial ideas, was consigned to a private sphere and an interior world with which there could be little interaction. In many respects, this materialistic inheritance is still with us. It is seen in the reduction of love to sex, in the fear of suffering and death and in the endemic greed on which the present system depends.

That such views are still current is shown by a recent publication of the well-known novelist, Salman Rushdie. This is in the form of a letter written to the hypothetical six-billionth inhabitant of the earth. In it Rushdie urges this person to give up any thought of religious belief and any hope of heaven. What you see is what you get and it is futile to speculate about what we cannot know. Now it may take one boy from Karachi to see through another! There are three questions I would like to ask of Rushdie: first, he claims that because there was no 'churning' of the great pot at creation nor 'vomiting' of the galaxies – because the world was not literally created in six days, as we understand them, with the seventh as a day of rest – therefore, there is no such thing as creation. In other words, if you discount the 'mythological' language used by people in the past to describe creation, you have to give up the notion of creation itself! This is a somewhat strange position to adopt. Does it mean that Rushdie does not believe in the reality of the self simply because people in the past have described it in ways not agreeable to us? There seems to be a classic confusion between the reality and the language used by different ages to describe that reality. There is also an arrogance about the 'definitive' or 'final' nature of our own understanding and language. What is Rushdie's own account of the universe, if any?

Secondly, he urges this hapless person to exalt 'mind over dogma', but the mind seems to be a kind of *tasula rasa*, a blank slate, without context or tradition and without any principles to inform it in its decision-making. I am strongly reminded here of G K Chesterton's comment that the only point in having an open mind is to close it again on something fairly solid! Does not having a mind, which is genuinely seeking for truth, lead to the very asking of those ultimate questions about existence and destiny that Rushdie is so concerned to disallow?

His third point is that morals are free standing: that is, they do not relate to any religious or philosophical system, but have to do with 'endless conversations'. Well-known novelists may have the time for such conversations, but most people do not. In fact, history has shown us that religious belief and practice can support, strengthen and clarify our moral commitment. What then is the basis for moral decisions, for respecting human dignity, for faithfulness in relationships, for justice in society?

Another 'big story' that sometimes co-exists with modernism is what has come to be called postmodernism. The development of technology since the dawn of the modern era, the insistence on personal liberty from the time of the Reformation (now separated from a lively faith in God, which the reformers believed to be essential for the proper exercise of liberty), and the consigning of religion to the private sphere in the course of the Enlightenment have all conspired to produce a situation where the spiritual is seen more and more as individual, private and selective.[10]

This can lead directly to the denial that there is any overarching 'big story' at all that might give structure and meaning to our existence or, more indirectly, to the claim that we do not have means of discernment when confronted with the claims of several 'big stories'.[11] In the end, this means that there can be no worldview that commands the allegiance of all or even of many. There are two main consequences of such a position: there is an increasing emphasis on spirituality being for self-fulfilment rather than the common good (not least within the churches themselves) and there is the relativising of spiritual experience and insight. As the popular song puts it, 'You tell me your truth and I will tell you mine!' It has been pointed out, of course, that the denial of the possibility of a 'big story' to support our experience, and the claim that it is impossible to judge between the big stories in terms of truth and relevance, are themselves 'big stories' that are trying to gain our allegiance. Holding to such views will determine our view of the world no less than holding to another big story.

We live then in a context where the worldview and values espoused by religion continue to be marginalised from the public arena and where the rules of discussion exclude any acceptance of a common moral or spiritual framework. At the same time, highly individualised and private spiritualities that can be therapeutic and even provide people with a sense of direction for their lives are spreading like wildfire, but these have few consequences for society and make few moral demands on the individual. This may, of course, explain their popularity. As a young college student who had decided against confirmation said to me, 'At art college I am having a really cool time – won't that stop if I become a Christian?' The answer to that, of course, is 'no', or perhaps 'not necessarily', but she brought to mind another Chesterton saying: 'Christianity has not been tried and found wanting; it has been found difficult and not tried!' People are now increasingly aware of the spiritual, but they want spirituality without the personal and social demands of the Christian faith.

The shape of the world

The shapes of the church to come and its mission and ministry will continue to be affected by the shape of the world as it is now and as it will be in the future. Social scientists, such as Dr Grace Davie, have considered the complex relationship between believing and belonging in today's world. Not surprisingly, they have discovered a widespread reluctance to belong to any organisation that demands active participation. This includes voluntary organisations and political parties as well as the churches. While people are reluctant to belong to specific congregations, and while even denominational allegiance is crumbling, the surveys continue to show the persistence of belief and, sometimes, quite orthodox Christian belief. This has been characterised as 'believing without belonging'. It is important, however, to recognise that Dr Davie herself writes of 'drifting belief', and scholars like Professor Robin Gill hold that while belief persists it also mutates so that it becomes more and more selective and syncretistic. This is, indeed, borne out by the way in which both folk and civic religion are changing from their vaguely Christian basis to a pick 'n' mix mentality. For the former, this is shown in rites of passage where people are increasingly insistent on making up their own wedding, funeral, and even christening services – even when the church is involved. In our part of the world, Frank Sinatra's 'I did it my way' seems to be a runaway favourite at funerals!

In civic religion there is pressure, of course, to acknowledge in some way the presence of people belonging to other world faiths.[12] There is also a growing sense, however, that Christianity should not be allowed exclusive expression, because having a number of expressions increases tolerance and enriches the community.

While Grace Davie has shown how believing can persist without active belonging, Robin Gill makes us aware of those who try to belong even when they no longer believe. The mission of the church needs to ensure maximum acceptance so that people find it easy to belong, as well as planned programmes of learning and nurture so that commitment is strengthened and faith deepened.[13]

Moving from behaviour to currents of thought, at least two opposite movements are discernible here. On the one hand, the tradition of criticism and analysis that characterised the 'modern' is continuing also in the postmodern. Not only texts but persons are viewed as having their own axes to grind and thus as worthy of hermeneutical suspicion. Continual questioning of the motives, integrity and distinctiveness of founding figures erodes reverence for such figures and jeopardises their authority. This is not to deny a proper place for historical and literary research but if 'suspicion' becomes the sole underpinning for it, it will create a crisis in meaning and, perhaps, lead to a comprehensive disenchantment in society (as modernism has done). Bereft of tradition and its authority, people will be unable to recognise 'signals' of transcendence when they come across them.

Such attitudes sit uneasily with the professed openness to mystery and wonder also seen as characteristic of our postmodern world. People are becoming more and more open to ways of knowing that are not restricted to sense experience and reflection upon it or to logic and mathematics. They are more receptive to intuition, mystical knowledge and holistic ways of knowing. Many bookshops now have whole sections devoted to these special ways of 'knowing'. The space devoted to conventional religion compares very poorly with these newer sections. Even the broadsheet newspapers are now willing to run stories of people who have had some kind of mystical experience without having had any religious background.

Some scientists who are not always sympathetic to religion are acknowledging the mystery of the universe. The well-known campaigner for a Darwinian worldview, Professor Richard Dawkins of the University of Oxford, in his Dimbleby lecture concentrated his attention on science as a vehicle for expressing the wonder and the mystery of the universe. This is moving well beyond the attitudes of his philosophical predecessors who took science to be about 'problem solving'. I had to respond to his lecture the next day on the *Today* radio programme and asked him if such views represented a convergence between Darwinian scientists and religion. He replied that he was against all religion but if we had to have religion, Christianity was preferable to some other options that are around these days.

There is a dilemma here for the church, or is it a double opportunity? On the one hand, Christians believe that the *Logos* (the eternal Word), incarnate as Jesus of Nazareth, is the rational principle that orders the universe and provides it with coherence. They believe also that the *Logos* illumines all human beings (John 1:1–18). They are not surprised, therefore, that there is a correspondence between the human mind and the world it wishes to observe. Again, for them faith as a way of believing and trusting, based on what has happened in the world and has been experienced by human beings, is open to investigation from a variety of angles: historical, literary, ethical and psychological. To put it simply, faith must have the consent of reason.

On the other hand, believers are only too aware that humans are finite creatures and cannot encompass all the mysteries of the universe, let alone the mystery of God's being. Belief in a transcendent source for the world's order and beauty may be logical but that does not reduce the transcendent itself to the merely logical. Christians are sympathetic, therefore, towards those who emphasise the wonder and the mystery of the universe.

In other words, Christians can communicate with those who emphasise the importance of inquiry: scientific, historical or literary. At the same time, they have much in common with those who give priority to the 'beyondness' of the spiritual and the immediate impact it can make on us. Facing both ways, in this sense, will remain important for the mission of the church to come.

The spiritual and the moral

We have considered the problems and difficulties which the church will continue to face but there are positive factors too in the emerging context of the twenty-first century. I have mentioned one already: the increasingly widespread recognition that *spirituality* is not a 'virus' we acquire from our social context but is 'deep-wired' into our psyches. There seems to be more and more evidence of the innateness of a spiritual sense. Alongside this, 'spirituality' is no longer a taboo term, but is freely discussed and, in some circles, is actually a fashionable buzzword.

The background to this new status for spirituality goes back to the work of groups like the Alister Hardy Institute in Oxford during the 1970s and 1980s, which sought to place the investigation of spiritual experience on a scientific level. One study found that a significant proportion of 'working-men', at some point in their lives, had gone through a definite spiritual experience. The study also discovered, however, that they had been unable to talk about it and so the experience was never socialised. Those familiar with male culture of a certain kind will readily recognise that discussion on religion is not encouraged in the pub, the club or the shop floor. This has meant that people's experience has remained with them – it has not been shared – and thus there has been little growth either for those who have had the experience or for their colleagues.

More recent researchers, like David Hay and Kate Hunt of the University of Nottingham, have confirmed the existence of widespread, if somewhat diffuse, spirituality, even when it has little to do with organised religious practice.[14] Hay and another collaborator, Rebecca Nye, have shown also that children are innately spiritual and, furthermore, rather than 'learning' spirituality from adults, it is often from them that they 'unlearn' it or, at least, are discouraged from talking about it.[15] Naturally, if such a thesis is true this has enormous implications for our educational approach, not just in terms of collective worship in schools or worship in church but the way in which we approach religious education, whether in schools or in church. We cannot just leave children with a superficial 'comparative' examination of different beliefs and practices, not even with a discussion of important moral issues, but, somehow, we need to engage their hearts as well as their minds.

This awareness of the spiritual, diffuse yet widespread (universal?), is a huge challenge to Christians who have the means to express their own spirituality in terms of ritual, symbol and communal living. Each of these is extremely important as far as our missionary response is concerned. While recognising and respecting the spirituality of those around us, we need to communicate all that God has done in Christ in ways that are accessible to the various cultural groups in our plural environment.

If spirituality is seen as innate, there is also a growing sense that *morality* is innate. While sociobiology is taking things too far in seeing moral behaviour as concerned exclusively with the survival of the species, our own nature and that of our environment do suggest to us ways of behaving that make for personal, social and ecological flourishing, and others that do not. We have, however, to beware of deriving 'ought' entirely from 'is', and part of moral awareness has to do with transcending nature when it does not correspond to our knowledge of the 'good' required of us. Either way, it cannot be denied that human beings have a fundamental moral capacity that leads to the recognition of moral principles understood as being universal in scope. (In this sense, there can be no 'tribal' morality; simply a greater or lesser awareness of a moral principle in a particular age or culture.) Moral judgements may themselves be spontaneous but, at the same time, they are informed by moral principles. Also, our moral character develops as we deliberate about what we are to do and reflect on what we have done. All of this moral activity is related to the recognition of a universal moral order, or moral law, which Professor Oliver O'Donovan defines as 'that wisdom which contains insight into the created order when it is formulated explicitly to direct decisions'.[16] Some call it 'natural law' even though that term is widely misunderstood. Pope John Paul II, in his encyclical *Veritatis Splendor*, calls it the 'eternal law' impressed on every man or woman.[17] Others refer to moral awareness as an aspect of our natural development.

Whatever it is called, it bears witness to the mutuality between ourselves and the ordered world in which we are called to live. This mutuality informs our judgements and allows dialogue with others about the world in which we live, our society and our own personal destinies.

Richard Holloway, former Bishop of Edinburgh, seems to be correct, then, in his claim that it *is* possible to make moral judgements, to engage in moral dialogue about the common good and about our own flourishing without an explicit appeal to revelation and, indeed, with people like Salman Rushdie who would disallow such an appeal.[18] This much appears to be true but, of course, it is not sufficient. What then is lacking in such a thesis? Obviously, revelation bears witness to the universal moral law. Left to ourselves we may want to deny aspects of such a moral law, or to deny it altogether, but revelation directs us back to it.

Secondly, revelation *clarifies* what may be obscure or imperfectly grasped. It *confirms* what conscience knows already and it can *correct* where conscience has gone wrong. We must not underestimate this possibility. Not only does conscience have to be formed and educated in its understanding of basic principles; it may also have to be corrected when it has either failed to grasp a principle or has misapplied it. The continual 'reformation of manners' that should characterise every Christian life takes place under the direction of revelation.

Finally, revelation shows us that we cannot keep the moral law in our own strength. We need the power and the love of God to do this and are assured of his forgiveness when we fall short but are repentant, wish to make good what we have damaged and want to start again. Our freedom consists in our conduct having its wellsprings in the love of Christ, which frees us from empty legalism and yet provides us with a frame of reference. Because of love we can be forgiven and make a new start.[19]

Recall, repentance and reconciliation

Greater awareness of the spiritual and the moral are certainly 'attachment points' in the contemporary scene with which the gospel can be connected, but we know also that we do not live in a perfect world. True, there is beauty, intricacy, balance and order in the universe around us and within us, but there is also fragility, cruelty and waste. Any properly Christian account of the universe will have to engage with *both* of these aspects of our world – that is to say, we must engage with order and beauty, but we dare not ignore the more chaotic element of the world in which we live.[20]

For our purposes, however, we need to focus on both the reality and the potential of human evil. While the churches have been soft-pedalling traditional Christian teaching in this area, there is a vigorous discussion going on in literature and the arts. The great novelist William Golding is a well-known example of dealing with seemingly radical evil. At a more popular level, and in a different way, we have the works of storytellers like Stephen King. His novels are powerful and rich studies of the evil that exists outside in the world, but also of the way it flourishes within human beings. King recognises human powerlessness to withstand radical evil. Only the grace of God, working in persons, can equip the human race for the struggle against sin, disease, social division and internal anger. For a long time now,

King has known that only a miracle can save us. In a similar way Golding's biographer, Peter Medcalf, in his obituary tells us that Golding believed humanity to be both heroic *and* sick.[21] Even in the depths of degradation there is the horizon of the divine, and hidden behind the darkness is that light which Golding himself calls God. In spite of appearances, there is a profound (and benevolent) mystery at the heart of the universe of which we can be made aware.

Modern art is often about the felt void of silence and darkness – a refusal to see meaning in any aspect of our existence – or it can also be about the ways in which the structures of society conceal rottenness, decay and the predatory in our nature. [22] Both literature and art, then, reveal to us an aspect of the human condition that resonates strongly with the analysis of the Bible. It is true that we are made in God's image and have the possibility of recalling our authentic purpose and destiny, but it is true also that the image has been damaged and obscured in us and that we have lost our way. Instead of forging ahead on the spiritual and moral pathways set out for us in terms of our true nature, we tend again and again to revert to the merely 'animal' in us. One view of original sin, which has been popular among some scientists who are Christians, is that it has to do with our inherited animal nature that seeks continually to dominate our spiritual and moral consciousness. However, it is not animal nature as such that is sinful, but our capitulation to it in spite of awareness of the higher demands our spiritual nature and conscience make upon us. Our animal nature does, however, provide the conditions for sinning.[23] In terms jof such an analysis, it is not only the possibility of 'recall' that is important but of repentance so that we can, once again, lay hold of our divinely given destiny.

The question of repentance, however, brings to the fore the extent to which we are caught in the coils of our own rebellion. Martin Luther's language may sound exaggerated to twenty-first century ears, but his analysis is essentially sound: we are so bound by our social and personal sinfulness that we cannot, of ourselves, escape from it.[24] Although the origins of this bondage lie in the rebellion of the will, every aspect of human life and nature has been affected by it. For this reason, while fragmented knowledge of the true and the good is possible and we can also experience love and friendship in a partial way, we need rescue if we are to recover the original wholeness intended for us.

The divine initiative, then, is absolutely fundamental if we are to recover our original purpose. It is here that we rely so much on revelation. Of course, there can be a sense of the divine work through creation and conscience, but as we come to know how God has acted among a particular people, in specific historical circumstances, we can appreciate the range of the divine plan and the depth of divine love. Any fragmentary experience of God is then made whole and deepened through its contact with revelation. Later on, we shall have opportunity to see how the continuity of spiritual experience, even of revelation, relates to the once-for-allness of God's saving acts as recorded in the Bible.

Fundamental to a Christian understanding of this divine initiative is God's desire to reconcile us to the divine life. In spite of human waywardness, salvation history is all about God's work in ending our alienation. Atonement or 'at-one-ing' has, after all, this primary meaning. It is focused most sharply, definitively we can say, in the coming, the working, the suffering and the dying of Jesus of Nazareth. The earliest Christian testimony saw this as the person, the place and the time when God's offer to us of recovery and return is most clearly made. This is inescapable, even if it has to be related to how God acts throughout history.

Because of God's action we can respond and acknowledge that the world and our lives have meaning. We can know that love is at the heart of the universe and that, in spite of appearances, the world has a benevolent purpose in its existence. Such a realisation can be called 'peace with God'.

Alongside reconciliation with God, and flowing from it, is peace within ourselves, the need to deal with our own self-alienation and dis-ease. From the very beginning, Jesus' own ministry and the commission he gave first to the Twelve and then to the Seventy (or Seventy-Two) included the work of healing with prayer and anointing with oil (Mark 6:7–13 and parallels; Luke 10:9; Mark 9:29; cf. James 5:13–16). Taking their cue from the eucharistic teaching in St John's Gospel (e.g. ch 6), many Christian traditions have seen the Eucharist or the Supper of the Lord as a place for and a means of healing for body, soul and spirit. Ignatius, writing to churches in Asia on his way to martyrdom in Rome, early in the second century, refers to it as the 'medicine of immortality' (*Pharmakon Athanasias*) and as an 'antidote' for our preservation in Christ.[25] This theme is maintained throughout history and can be characterised by the remark of the Scottish reformer, John Knox, that the Lord's Supper is 'a singuler medicine for all poore sicke creatures'.[26]

Many clergy, with lay teams and centres dedicated to the promotion of a healing ministry, continue this work of healing, sometimes alongside medical and other assistance. Apart from prayer, anointing and other sacramental means, the church seeks to continue its task of healing through support for medical and surgical ways of dealing with illness. Hospital chaplains are concerned for the whole person and for wholeness in a hospital's approach to patients. They are involved not only with patients but with staff in support and advice at times of great stress and when difficult medical and ethical decisions have to be made. In addition to the general care they provide, hospital chaplains need to be seen, more and more, as experts who make a distinctive contribution to the care of the ill.

A great deal of healing work is done, however, in the pastor's study or its equivalent, when properly trained lay people are also involved. Pastoral care has always been seen as part of the work of those who have leadership in the church (1 Peter 5:1–4). In the early period it grew greatly because of an increasing need to provide penitential discipline for Christians. Since then it has been associated with listening to those with troubled consciences, guiding them with God's word, strengthening the weak and bringing reconciliation in situations of inner or social conflict. Pastoral care, in this context, needs always to be informed by God's love as it is seen in creation and redemption. Out of this emerges a distinctively Christian anthropology which recognises that people are made in God's image, that they have the ability to recall that they are 'fearfully and wonderfully made', but, also, that they can realise how far they have fallen short of God's purpose for them – as it is revealed in the proclamation of the gospel. This brings about repentance and a desire to be right with God, right within and right with others.

These days pastoral care can also be informed by one or more of the psychological frameworks that have become available for therapeutic work. Whether these are psychodynamic, analytical or behavioural, care needs to be taken that the methods used are consonant with the gospel. There may well be insights from various models about the nature of the human personality, its development and ways in which behaviour can be modified that are useful for pastoral work but they should always be rigorously examined against an authentically biblical view of the human condition.

Because of the element of guidance and spiritual direction in pastoral care, there will always be a tension between it and formal counselling, which is usually non-directive. For these and other reasons, pastors may wish to refer people for counselling to someone else. It is important that their pastoral and evangelical role is not compromised. Another area of tension has to do with the balance of priorities between therapeutic work with individuals and the demands of the church and the wider community. Group therapy and other means are sometimes employed to ease this tension but, in the end, pastors should be aware of the importance of community for the wholeness of the person. Our personalities are shaped not only by our parents and our earliest experiences but also by the wider community. Reconciliation, restoration and a sense of wholeness, likewise, can come through properly mediated interaction with the community. As the African concept of *Ubuntu* has it, 'I am because we are', and the wholeness of the community is crucial to my wholeness. Pastoral care and even counselling, under Christian auspices, will never be about just sweeping things under the carpet and helping people simply to come to terms with their situation. There has to be an element of the desire to put things right. Issues of justice may emerge that need to be addressed prophetically, or particular kinds of need may be revealed for which provision will have to be made. An obvious example is when pastoral care or counselling reveals situations of domestic violence. This is not just a matter of helping a person to cope with a situation. Outside the confines of a particular case, the church may have to campaign for greater awareness in society, for the involvement of the social services and of law-enforcement agencies. Christians and churches may also become involved in the provision of 'refuges' and other means of support.

The churches' long-term and widespread involvement in healing is, at last, being acknowledged by others. A recent report by the Mental Health Education Council acknowledges the place of spirituality in addressing mental illness. This is a change from the usual position that spiritual experience is *part* of the illness, to a position that spirituality may help in its treatment. There are numerous examples of spiritual experience or belief helping people who have been at the point of complete mental and nervous breakdown to reintegrate their own lives and even to function well in the community. In *The Search for Faith,* we quoted Dr Oliver Sacks' story of a profoundly amnesiac man who was helped to recollect himself at the Eucharist. Here was an act that involved his whole being and had a continuity that even his trauma was unable to fracture.[27] The World Health Organisation too is at the point of completing an international and cross-cultural survey which will show that spirituality helps people to keep well and to recover more quickly when they do get ill. The WHO will be recommending that spirituality should become one of the criteria for assessing the well-being of communities and persons. Many physicians and medical journals too are more sympathetic to religious practice as they can see its benefits in healthy lifestyles and better recovery rates.

Just as peace with God leads to a process of healing within ourselves, so it should lead to the breaking down of barriers within the fellowship of believers. In Galatians 3:28 St Paul sets out not only his view of an egalitarian church but also what amounts to a fundamental anthropology or doctrine of humanity: 'There is neither Jew nor Greek, slave nor free, male nor female, for you are all one in Christ Jesus.' This thinking is echoed in passages like Colossians 3:11 and Ephesians 2:11f. It is the basis for the church's universal mission and also for the emergence of a new kind of community in the ancient world. Whatever else we may want to say about Paul's teachings regarding women and men, Jews and Gentiles, slaves and free, they are governed by this fundamental way of seeing things.

Social commentators have often pointed out that one of the reasons for the rapid growth of the early church was that, within it, all the most important barriers of the ancient world were broken down.[28] The social barriers, for instance, between Jew and Gentile based on Jewish dietary laws or the barriers between men and women at worship or in the home. Many have pointed out the mutuality that is required of all in the so-called household codes.[29] The barriers between the free and slaves – what a fundamental barrier that was – had to be overcome. Even Aristotle calls slaves 'living tools', and yet in the church there was no distinction in the Liturgy between slave and free. All the church's offices (including that of bishop) were open to slaves and the church played such an important role in the improvement of the condition of slaves and in their manumission (purchase of their freedom from the common fund) that the emperor Constantine, after his conversion, gave the church special privileges in this respect.[30] When the social reformers of the eighteenth and nineteenth centuries, like William Wilberforce, began their struggle against slavery, there was already considerable Christian thought and practice behind them, not least in the New Testament itself.

Our own peace with God, within ourselves and in the believing community, should be the fuel that drives the engine of mission to the world. It is, indeed, as the distinguished Sri Lankan D T Niles has said, a case of one beggar telling another where to find bread. A church that recognises difference but does not discriminate because of it will be more able to bring peace to the world's conflicts.

At the height of the civil war in Bosnia I went there on behalf of Christian Aid to see if we could work together with some of the Islamic relief organisations in delivering relief to all those in need and not just to those of our confession. At one point we were taken to Nagorny Vaquf, a town at the centre of some of the most horrible massacres during that particularly bloody conflict. I was shown the road that divided the communities and was told how the Muslims knew very well the Serbs who had killed their relatives, and vice versa. Even indirect negotiations seemed very distant and yet, in the middle of that extremely tense and violent situation, there was a small Christian community working for reconciliation! One could not find a more unpromising mission field (and, believe me, I have seen a few) but the Easter faith makes the Easter people do some strange things. The San Egidio community, based in Rome, but working all over the world, were able to broker a peace in another civil war – that in Mozambique – because, according to their own testimony, they were the only group who had no arms, no power and no money. This is one of the reasons why they were trusted on all sides. There is still a lot to say for the powerlessness of the Christian missionary.

These are, of course, two rather dramatic stories but in our own context volunteers from the churches continue to work away quietly in organisations like the mediation schemes and Victim Support seeking to bring about a resolution of conflict, without recourse to the police or the courts. Their work is equally important in bringing the gospel to bear on life today.

We began with the question 'Is there a gospel for the twenty-first century?' and we have tried to outline an answer to that question in this chapter. I have suggested that the answer is to be found in our interaction with the 'big stories' of our time, with a recognition of the innateness of both spirituality and morality, with taking seriously the dark side of human nature and with the gospel's capacity to heal us and to restore those basic relationships that allow human beings to flourish. Our next question must be 'What should be the shape of a church that seeks to bring such a gospel to such a world?'

2. Is There a Future for the Church?

CASE STUDY

Charis is reading a one-year Bible that helps her to get through the whole Bible in the course of a year. As she reads about wars, cruelty, the place of women and ancient views of the universe, she begins to ask herself, 'What on earth has this to do with me?' Her pastor tells her simply to believe that the Bible is the word of God and is relevant to every age. The local library, on the other hand, has a book that tells her how the Bible is the product of ancient societies and treats it like it would any other kind of ancient literature. Does the Bible have anything to say to Charis and her friends? How is she to hear God's word today? How important is the Bible in today's church?

The shape of the church is determined not only by the shape of the world. What people believe, how they belong, their values and their relationships are all, of course, important in shaping the structures, language and ministry of the church, but that is not the whole story: there is an inner dynamic that is important too. Something essential in the nature of the church influences, indeed determines, its shape in every age and every culture. However responsive the church may be to outside pressures, there is an internal dynamic that must be taken into account.

The church is shaped by the faith

This inward pressure is nothing other than the handing on and the receiving of the gospel, 'the whole counsel of God', from age to age, from culture to culture and from community to community. In 1 Corinthians 15, for example, St Paul writes of delivering to the church at Corinth what he himself had first received; that is, an account of Holy Week, the death, burial and resurrection appearances of the Lord. In 1 Corinthians 11, similarly, he speaks of delivering the teaching about the Lord's Supper that he had received from the Lord. In 2 Thessalonians 2 he exhorts the Christians there to stand firm by the traditions, both oral and written, that he had taught them.

St Paul is an interesting example of the receiving and handing on of the faith. On the one hand, he had a direct and tremendous experience of the risen Lord at the time of his conversion. His personal relationship with the Lord comes through again and again. It also influenced his view of the church as the body of Christ and of the Eucharist as the presence of the Lord in his body the church. On the other hand, when Paul recounts the essentials of the faith, as in 1 Corinthians 15, he uses the language of *paradosis*, 'Tradition' or 'passing on'. Even in 1 Corinthians 11, when he speaks of passing on what he has received from the Lord, commentators are agreed that this is likely to mean a reference not only to the historical Jesus as the originator of Tradition but also to the exalted Lord who is the real author of the whole tradition developing within the apostolic church. In this sense, what is received from the apostolic witness is also of the Lord.[1] St Paul is not, of course, the only New Testament writer to emphasise the importance of Tradition. The letters in the name of Peter and the letter of Jude also give it a central place in their teaching.

You will have noticed that I have been spelling 'Tradition' with a capital 'T'. This is to distinguish apostolic Tradition, or the faith 'once for all delivered to the saints', from the customs, practices, ways of worship, and so on, that have emerged in the various Christian churches, sometimes as a response to the gospel and at other times as a distortion of it. Part of the church's calling as *semper reformanda* (ever reforming) is both to examine carefully its traditions in the light of the apostolic witness and also to be sure that Christians are faithful to it.

Scripture and tradition

The first generation of Christians knew what was truly apostolic because they heard it from the mouths of the apostles themselves or from their closest companions, and they read of it in letters and other works written by these people. But how do *we* know what is truly apostolic? This is a much more difficult question to answer. The different churches have, for good or ill, developed different traditions of their own. Over the course of time many have adapted to, or even compromised with, the culture around them. As the Articles of Religion say, some of their practices arise out of 'a corrupt following of the apostles'.[2] In such a complex situation, how are we to identify the 'Great Tradition' coming down from the apostles themselves? Here the church has felt the need for a canon or norm that would help it to decide what was authentically apostolic. The early Christians continued to read the Bible of the Jewish people whether in Hebrew, Greek or Aramaic paraphrase. Although there were some challenges to this practice, it was agreed that the church could not understand the life, death and resurrection of Christ and her own calling and mission without reference to the Jewish Bible. Already, during the period in which the books of the New Testament were being written, the writings of the apostles and their companions were coming to be recognised as Scripture (2 Thessalonians 2:15; 2 Peter 3:15–16). There were, of course, external criteria for recognition of the apostolic books as Scripture. These included authorship within the apostolic circle and transmission in the communities founded by the apostles or their companions. The 'rule of faith', the church's essential confession and the apostolic books were mutually interdependent: the rule of faith allowed the church to discern what was Scripture, and Scripture, in turn, determined the form and content of the rule of faith.

It is sometimes claimed that it took three or four centuries to agree the Canon finally. This is true, but a couple of points need to be made straight away. First of all, it is the word 'finally' that is important here. Many of the central books of the New Testament were recognised from the beginning as authentic but there was debate about some, such as the letter to the Hebrews and Revelation. Others, like the letter of Barnabas, just failed to be included. Indeed, that the matter is not closed even now can be seen from the fact that the Ethiopian Orthodox Church includes certain books in its canon not included by other churches. Secondly, the church did not see itself as creating a canon but as recognising the authority of what was there already.[3]

The church has always seen Scripture as a reliable record of how God has acted among his people and in his world and, equally important, how people have *perceived* the divine action and understood the divine intention. The arrival of biblical criticism in its modern form has certainly shown us the complexity of the biblical material, its convoluted history and the ways in which authors and editors have shaped the narratives for their own purposes and to meet their own needs. In spite of this, however, a sense of the transcendent world breaking into the mundane remains and distinguishes the Bible from other literature.

Because the authors, compilers and editors wrote, naturally, in their own cultural, scientific and literary contexts, the concerns, challenges and commitments of the Bible have to be reinterpreted to our own age and culture so that they may be understood and a response made possible. The task of the critic is to open us up to the worlds in which the Bible was first written. For this the critic needs not only the resources of literary and historical criticism but also those provided, for example, by the sciences of archaeology and anthropology. The tasks of the theologian, commentator and preacher, however, include a creative interpretation and application of the Bible's concerns and challenges to our own situation.

Scripture is inspired and inspiring

Of course, Scripture is not *merely* a record. Its enduring capacity to bring 'the beyond into our midst' gives it the quality of being inspired or God-breathed (the New Testament uses a very distinctive term, *theopneustos*, in 2 Timothy 3:16 to refer to Scripture's 'inspiration', but, in truth, it assumes this inspiration everywhere).[4] Such a view need not bind us to 'mechanical' or 'verbal' theories of inspiration. The writers' skills, gifts and limitations are not put in abeyance for inspiration to work. It is, rather, that they are transcended. The diversity of the material in the Bible is, at first sight, simply breathtaking. Alongside the literary quality of the book of Job are the historical books. The sophistication of St John's Gospel or of the so-called catholic letters co-exists with the earthiness of St Mark and the symbolism of the book of the Revelation. Yet there is an underlying unity about God's love, his purposes and how he is fulfilling them, even through the rejection and rebellion of his own creation and in suffering and sacrifice. The language and style have to be held in tension with the divine disclosure made through them. Commentators tell us again and again how the style of a passage and its language are characteristic of the author, but they immediately go on to point out that this does not exhaust the sense of the passage. The words and style may be distinctive but they may refer back to an older tradition or to events widely acknowledged to have occurred. They may, indeed, mediate the divine.[5]

I have often referred to the conversation Henry Martyn, the famous Bible translator and missionary, had with the prime minister in Persia (Iran as it is now). The prime minister had explained what Muslims believed about the Qur'an; he then asked Martyn what Christians believed about the Bible. Martyn's reply is illuminating: 'the sense is from God but the expression from the different writers of it'. Martyn was greatly influenced in this and other matters by Charles Simeon, the great evangelical vicar of Holy Trinity, Cambridge, and his reply has affinities with other leading evangelicals of this time, such as Philip Doddridge.[6] Such views allow us to see that the Bible, as a whole, is inspired without requiring that the literary forms and words used by the authors and editors come directly from God. It is, rather, God using the language, knowledge and skills of human beings, partial though they might have been, to convey his truth and grace through them.

Scripture, however, is not just inspired in terms of its own character; it is also *inspiring* in the effect it has on those who read it, preach from it and seek to live their lives by it. It has long been recognised that the Bible has inspired writers and artists sometimes in ways that can be regarded as formative of culture. A great deal of poetry, music, sculpture and painting has been inspired by biblical stories and themes. Nor is this a matter simply of the past. The success of the millennial *Seeing Salvation* exhibition at the National Gallery has shown us the extent to which people are still capable of being moved by great spiritual themes interpreted by great artists. The Christian artist Anthony Green's sculpture for the millennium is a contemporary expression of Christian faith and hope in the midst of life's real problems. For him, in the concreteness of the family, as well as in its fragility, the continuity of affection and the persistence of love are most clearly observed.[7]

The capacity of Scripture to inspire is not, of course, seen only in works of art or of literature. It is (and should be) seen in all of Christian endeavour. In our contribution to the political and social questions of today, as well as our approach to moral and spiritual guidance, Scripture should be the informing principle.[8] In terms of daily living also Scripture continues to inspire men and women to remain faithful, to give sacrificially of their time and money, to be prepared to suffer and, sometimes, even to die for the sake of the gospel. What, then, is the relation of Scripture to the church's great Tradition?

In the past, this matter has, sometimes, caused considerable controversy. Some have held, for example, that there are two sources of divine revelation: Scripture and Tradition, each having its own autonomy. Others have held that Scripture is primary and Tradition, such as it is, must be subordinate to it. Earlier in this chapter we saw how the authentic apostolic teaching was conveyed both in writing and orally – the two forms being seen in the New Testament as neither isolated nor autonomous from one another, but as related. The question of the norm has, however, remained and the church's recognition of the Canon of Holy Scripture is significant at this point. Holy Scripture is not something in addition to Tradition, nor is Tradition something in addition to Scripture. One is not set against the other. Rather, we may say, Scripture is part of the continuing flow of apostolic Tradition in the teaching, preaching and worshipping life of the church. It is part of it, but it is the *normative* part. That is to say, Scripture allows us to discern what is authentically apostolic. It is the touchstone by which we may determine what is part of the great Tradition of the church, even if we allow that this Tradition has developed over the ages and has come to be expressed in a variety of ways.

As the recent report of the Anglican–Roman Catholic International Commission (ARCIC) has put it, 'Within Tradition the Scriptures occupy a unique and normative place and belong to what has been given once for all.'[9]

What Scripture affirms

To claim, however, that Scripture is the normative part of Tradition and helps to guarantee its authenticity, raises a number of questions about Scripture itself. Is everything in Scripture of equal value and of equal value today? Is, for instance, the history of Israelite settlement in Canaan of as much significance as the Ten Commandments and the devotion of the Psalms, or the passionate thirst for justice in some of the writing Prophets? How do we avoid 'proof-texting' and discern the mind of Scripture on a particular matter? Is there a 'canon' within the Canon to which we can appeal, or are there broad themes, such as creation, redemption, a biblical anthropology, which remain consistent and which can, therefore, provide guidance for us?

Another way of approach might be to consider what Scripture *affirms*. This implies that not everything in Scripture is necessary for faith and behaviour. Charles Simeon, although he held a very high view of biblical inspiration, allowed, nevertheless, that there were 'inexactnesses' in the Bible in relation to certain matters. Philip Doddridge and his friends even asked whether there were passages that provided a greater insight into the mind of God.

The Bible is a collection of books that are very different

from one another. They have been written, collated and edited over many centuries. They represent material that has originated in different languages and that addresses many different contexts. It would be very surprising, indeed, if the Bible did not contain material that can be regarded as incidental or relevant strictly to its original context. This should not, in any way, detract from the universality of the Bible's great themes and projects.

In discussion with Muslim friends we sometimes find ourselves comparing the Bible and the Qur'an. For all its complexity, the latter was completed in the lifetime of a single person, the Prophet of Islam. Even its later collation and standardisation did not take more than a generation.[10] This is completely different from the Bible and, among other things, should alert us to the difficulties inherent in comparison.

In asking what Scripture affirms or what the scope or mind of Scripture is, I am aware that Christians may come to different conclusions. It may, however, also be possible to identify some common elements that would command a wide area of agreement.

First of all, there is Scripture's insistence on discovering a reason and a plan for the universe. In other words, Scripture affirms *God the Creator*. The well-known scholar Gerhard von Rad in his commentary on the book of Genesis has pointed out that ancient Israel both took account of the best science available to it and interpreted it in the light of its own faith in Yahweh, the one God who was also Lord of the universe.[11] The science of the biblical writers, he goes on to say, may seem inaccessible or antiquated to us. Our task, however, is to tell the story of the creation in terms of the best science available to us. If acknowledging God as Creator is one of Scripture's central affirmations, what does that mean for the church today and how can we explain it to the world?

Professor John Polkinghorne (to take one example) has been pointing out for many years now that to say God is Creator in our world today is to say, among other things, that God is the source of the laws that govern the universe and that make science possible. Science assumes those laws and without them there would be no ordered world at all, and, therefore, no science! Nor are these laws simply an imposition of the human mind on the manifold of experience. There is certainly a correspondence between the human mind and the world as it is but the laws are not mere human inventions; they are deeply embedded in the structure of the universe in ways that allow us to discover them and to work with them.[12]

God may be seen, then, as the author of this finely tuned and balanced universe. Unlike John Polkinghorne, Bishop Hugh Montefiore is not a scientist, but some years ago he wrote a remarkable book called *The Probability of God*. In this book he meditates on the pictures of the universe that science is producing for us. The rate of its expansion, for example, is neither so fast that matter and energy dissipate into an endless void, nor so slow that the universe 'implodes' upon itself. 'Right' timing and the 'right' proportions of materials lead to the formation of the galaxies, stars and their planets. Without such 'fine-tuning' there would be no universe at all. But, Montefiore goes on to reflect, God is not only the author of a universe that has produced life; he is also the creator and sustainer of the systems that themselves sustain life and allow for its development. Here

Montefiore relies heavily on Jim Lovelock's *Gaia* hypothesis. This hypothesis has had a tremendous impact on environmentalists. It understands the earth (or *Gaia* in Greek) to be such a closely interrelated and interdependent system for the sustenance of life, that one can speak of the earth itself as an organism, as living. Whether the conclusion follows from the premises need not concern us here. It is certainly true that life does depend on a closely interdependent and delicately balanced world. Not only, however, is there a finely tuned and balanced universe with definite laws, not only are there life-sustaining systems, but there are *observers* of all of these processes. The emergence of consciousness must seem the final miracle of all. Here are 'products' of the universe who can reflect on that which has produced them![13]

Another central affirmation of the Bible is that of God as *Redeemer*. It is true that we have been made in God's image but, as we have seen, something has gone wrong as well. We are not what we have been made to be and called to be. Nor is the world as it should be. Human sin has wreaked the most terrible havoc on it. When I talk to people with a profound sense of evil in the world, they often refer to human evil, such as genocide, famine caused by war or greed, or some great technological catastrophe. Nor can we ignore natural evil: there is much waste, cruelty and imperfection in the world around us. Any adequate view of redemption will have to take account of how creation itself is part of God's redemptive purposes (Romans 8:18–25).

Christians can never be content with the fashionable view of religion as 'inexpressible sentiment'. They believe in a God who communicates, whether that is in the 'book' of the world, the testimony of our own hearts and consciences or the witness of his special people, the prophets and the saints. In the same way, they believe in a God who acts, and not merely as a watchmaker who, at the beginning, winds up the clock of the universe and then lets it run down, hoping that something remarkable will happen in between. No, as we have seen, God is not only the Creator at the beginning but must be seen to be the Creator throughout the process of creation and recreation. The Bible, however, also tells us that God acts in a different way: he acts in the course of history and in the lives of men, women and peoples. Such is the Bible's emphasis on this aspect of God's action that many have taken it to be characteristic of a biblical view.

Naturally, there are some who have difficulties with this. Some time ago, I was in dialogue on the radio with a Palestinian woman, who was a professor and a practising Muslim. She found it completely impossible to understand why God should choose a particular people. Now, I could see where she was coming from and, to some extent, I could sympathise with her. The history of God's chosen people is full of conflict, ambiguity, pride and even greed. In this, of course, they share in the fallenness of all humanity. God's choice, however, of a particular people is so that his universal purposes may be fulfilled. Again and again, already in the patriarchal narratives (e.g. Genesis 12) and throughout the Hebrew Bible (but especially in the Prophets), there is a sense that God has chosen Israel to fulfil his universal purposes. The God who acts to save his people, Israel, is the God who acts to save the world. This paradox of particular choice yet of universal purpose comes, of course, to a climax in the person and work of Jesus Christ.[14]

The incarnation is a fine picture of God working *inside*

creation. Through taking on the pain in the world, God's suffering love works patiently for the fulfilment of his purposes, and he continues to work even in the face of rejection. The cross is a graphic picture of this rejection, and yet the miracle is that it is also the beginning of humanity's recreation and renewal in the way of God. In Christ's obedience unto death is revealed the original calling and destiny of Adam and of Eve. The cross both *reveals* the extent of God's sacrificial love and, at the same time, our *restoration* in God's image.

Such a revelation of love and such a restoration can only be appropriated by a proper response to them. This is the basis of the Greek word *metanoia*, of turning again, of repenting. I am not one of those who believes that *anamnesis* (recall) and *metanoia* are opposites that must be kept apart. Anglican theology has been inclined to allow that *anamnesis* is a possibility for us – that to some extent, we are able to recall our original condition and calling, however much that may be affected by our fallenness. But that very awareness of who we are and what we are meant to be also shows us what we are not and what, in Christ, we can become. Recall, then, of Eden, of God's first intention for us, has to be held along with *repentance*: an acknowledgement that we have gone badly wrong and need to turn back to God, to his will for us and to the path that leads to our present and future well-being. As so often, George Herbert has summed it up well:

> In so much dregs the quintessence is small;
> The spirit and good extract of my heart
> Comes to about the many hundredth part
> Yet, Lord, restore thine image; hear my call
> And though my hard heart scarce to thee can groan
> Remember that thou once didst write in stone[15]

It is true, of course, that God's acts should not be confused with how people apprehended such acts, nor with metaphors, parables and stories that have been used to portray and to explain God's action. This is especially the case with all that happened on the cross. So often the imagery used about the transaction of the divine and human is confused with the reality itself. Metaphors are, of course, necessary: that of Christ as victor runs throughout the New Testament and beyond. In the early church this was understood as Christ's victory over the devil and all his angels. The vigour of this image does not, however, depend on any particular worldview or theory of evil. However evil is understood, such imagery of God's love coming into conflict with the hostile forces of evil and overcoming them through self-sacrifice will continue to make an impact.[16] 'Substitutionary' language may become distanced from images of a 'feudal' God needing satisfaction for offences against his dignity. It is still necessary, however, to speak of one standing in our place to do what we ought to do but cannot, and thus destroying the enmity between God and ourselves. As long as we continue to believe in the unity of humankind, it will be possible to speak of Christ as the one who is our 'representative', in his work both atoning for our sin and making a new start possible for all. Again, this language does not require a vengeful God who should be placated, but a sacrificial God who suffers with and for us.[17] However vigorous these metaphors remain and however they have been reinterpreted, God's work in Christ transcends them all and it is always possible to discover fresh metaphors, such as that of Eliot's 'wounded healer' or René Girard's 'innocent scapegoat' who exposes and undoes society's tendency to need scapegoats against whom we can all unite. Because of the one who has suffered outside the camp (Hebrews 13:12), we need not reinforce our corporateness by expelling those who threaten us.[18]

The whole of the Trinity is seen in Scripture as involved in the work of creation, redemption and sanctification. We do also, however, associate each of the Persons with one of these aspects of God's work in the world. If we associate the Father, for example, with creation, and the Son with redemption, it is natural to associate the Holy Spirit with the work of sanctification. Deuteronomy 30 and Romans 10 both emphasise the holiness of God's word and its capacity to make us holy. St John's Gospel, however, speaks of the Holy Spirit as showing the world the difference between right and wrong, strengthening moral integrity by enlivening our consciences and renewing our sense of justice or rightness (John 15:25–26; 16:7–8, 12–15). This Johannine sense of the Spirit's operation in the world is complemented by the Pauline awareness of the Spirit's work in the human person (1 Corinthians 2:14–16; 12:3; 2 Corinthians 3:4 – 4:6; Ephesians 1:17–20; 3:14–19). The Spirit is working to make us responsive to God's love and wisdom.

While the church in the West has generally emphasised the importance of God's word in the church and in the world, the Orthodox churches have generally stressed the *economy of the Holy Spirit*. For them, the Holy Spirit is not limited to the church or to the lives of Christian believers but is active in the world bringing people an awareness of what is right, of their own wrongdoing and its consequences, and converting people's hearts and minds to God, the source of all life and the saviour of all (1 Timothy 4:10). Such a view of the Holy Spirit's work has allowed the Orthodox to be more world-affirming and positive towards various human cultures, without compromising the historic faith of which they regard themselves as the custodians.[19]

What Scripture confirms

It will be obvious that Scripture's central affirmations about God have a profound impact on its understanding of the world and of the human condition: theology cannot for long be separated from anthropology, nor, indeed, from ecology.

Discerning what the Bible affirms provides us with a way of knowing what is vigorous in Tradition as a whole – its wellsprings as it were. The significance of Scripture is not, however, confined to what it affirms; it has also to do with what it *confirms*. How are we to understand this confirming role of the Bible? It is here that the Bible comes into a relationship with not only the received tradition of the church but also with human knowledge about the natural world and with the testimony of our conscience. What we know in creation and conscience is confirmed by Scripture. This is particularly so when we ask about *purpose*; the purpose or destiny of the human person, the reason for the family and wider communities and, in the end, the purpose of creation itself. As the great schoolman Thomas Aquinas has often said, the purpose is to be found in the original intention, even if it is achieved gradually. The original intention is God's and because God is good the final purpose is also good. This does not, in any way, imply a deterministic attitude towards the world and human beings. Part of the divine plan for the latter is precisely the possibility of acting freely and, even in the former, there is a degree of contingency. This means that the fulfilment of divine purpose is not the achievement of some pre-set plan but the development of the world and of human beings in ways most in accordance with their nature, and tending to maximise the good.[20]

Sometimes 'purpose' has been understood in a narrowly physiological sense, particularly in debates about human sexuality. This can be a blind alley into which 'natural law' thinking can sometimes lead. The questions need to be framed, rather, in terms of our whole relationship to God and to neighbour and then in terms of the purpose of sexuality, of the family and of the common good.[21] Asking questions like 'What is sexuality for?' 'What is the family for?' 'What is the common good?' does not, of course, imply that there are easy answers to any of these questions or that your answers and mine will necessarily agree in every detail. It is, however, important to ask such questions both in the light of Scripture and our knowledge of the world.

As we have seen, conscience is a capacity in us to tell right from wrong but it needs to be instructed and developed again, both in relation to our knowledge of what makes for natural, human and social flourishing and of the Scriptures that confirm such knowledge when it is authentically grounded and critically examined.

We have seen already how some Christians understand original sin. Another way of thinking about it is to hold that all of us have original sin because from the first moments of our existence we participate in the general human condition and context, which is systemically sinful. Such solidarity gives us an inclination to sin and leads, in fact, to actual sin.

This state of moral weakness, ignorance and culpability makes it important for us to have the guidance of revelation. Such guidance is not arbitrary. It has profoundly to do with how the world is made and how we are made and what makes for our wholeness and healing, as well as the world's.

How Scripture corrects

Again, because of our inherent sinfulness, the consequences of which remain even after the work of regeneration has begun, divine revelation is needed to *correct* whatever has gone wrong. At various times Christians, churches and movements have either compromised with the world's values and beliefs or, indeed, syncretised with other traditions or modes of thought and of life in ways that have not been authentic to apostolic Tradition as it is received from the Scriptures. At such times, the role of Scripture as the decisive rule of faith becomes important, if there is to be recovery and renewal.

In our ecumenical conversations we are discovering that when two or more Christian traditions (with a lower case 't') come together and acknowledge the common authority of the Bible, they discover where each has been faithful to the apostolic Tradition (capital 'T'), as well as compromises they have made along the way. Such discoveries lead to a new vision of the church, which should be the basis for genuine ecumenical agreement.

Looking at matters from another point of view, local churches and Christians naturally read the Scriptures in their own contexts with their various problems and opportunities. The context will lead them to notice certain stories in the

Bible or particular themes and emphases. It is well known how slaves in America understood their plight and their destiny in terms of the Exodus story. Women, similarly, have looked not only for role models but for feminine and maternal language about God in texts that admittedly come from largely patriarchal contexts. In the same way, Gentiles have sought God's universal purposes in books that often emphasise the particularity of the election of Israel. Each reading can be a faithful and valid reading of the Bible, but wise Christians and churches will see that their reading needs to be complemented by, and even from time to time corrected by, readings from other Christians and churches. If this happens in mutual Christian charity, the universal church will be able to retain a wholeness of view regarding its Bible.

Anglican moral and social thought takes the world seriously because of its incarnational basis. This strength can, however, become a weakness if we are led too much by experience of a particular situation, even, perhaps, involvement in it. It is right, of course, to take human weakness into account, but this should not become the basis of the church's guidance! That should, rather, be *informed* by what Scripture affirms and confirms about God, the world and ourselves. As we have seen, it is appropriate, indeed necessary, for us to take account of disciplines such as history, psychology and sociology in our approaches to contemporary issues, but this is additional to, not instead of, the need for us to inhabit the world of the Bible and for the Bible to permeate our thinking and our spirituality. It is necessary, then, to hold the Scriptures together with knowledge derived from other disciplines, while, at the same time, being clear that if there is a conflict between what has maturely and universally been determined as the 'mind of Scripture' and the presuppositions of or results derived from particular disciplines, the mind of Scripture will be definitive without foreclosing on further discussion of the issues.

We have seen, then, that the normative role of Scripture does not imply a mindless literalism about it. It is possible, indeed necessary, to take into account the different ways in which scholars have approached the Bible. We have seen that to acknowledge the human origins and history of the Scriptures need not be hostile to the divine sense mediated through them. The Scriptures function as a norm in the church and within the stream of Tradition, but such a functioning has also to do with how the faithful, and the church as a whole, discern the mind of Scripture: what the Bible affirms, confirms, corrects, informs and inspires.

Receiving and re-receiving

The Council of Jerusalem, held in AD 49, decided that gentile converts to Christian faith were not to be subjected to the rigours of the Mosaic law. This bold decision had far-reaching implications for the rapid spread of the Christian church in the gentile world of that time. It was, furthermore, of a piece with what we know of the Lord's teaching and practice. He too emphasised the importance of inward renewal over and above mere ritualistic cleansing (Mark 7:1–23). He looked beyond the letter of the law to its original intention in matters like marriage, divorce and adultery, in fraternal relations and in legal matters (Mark 10:1–12; Matthew 5:17–48; cf. 2 Corinthians 3:6). The insight of the Council of Jerusalem, that God shows no partiality but accepts all those who respond to Christ and seek to live by his moral and spiritual teaching, took a long time to be received by the church as a whole – as the pages of the New Testament bear witness. The teaching of the Council *was* radical but no more so than that of Paul and of Jesus himself.

Throughout the ages, the church has had to receive apostolic Tradition, including the Scriptures, in widely differing contexts, cultures and climes. Because of this, the receiving has sometimes to be a 're-receiving' (a term first employed by the Dominican Jean Tillard). In other words, there are moments in the life of a particular church, or of the whole church, when some aspect of Tradition has to be received in a new way because of changing circumstances, the arrival of the gospel among a new people or a new insight into the human condition. It may be that a known aspect of Tradition has to be examined in the light of fresh evidence, a forgotten part of it rediscovered or greater weight be put on a particular teaching.

In an African context, for example, often the biblical concern for wholeness is noticed. This may be because many African cultures see the human person as a psychosomatic unity, where the well-being of the soul cannot be separated from that of the body, or vice versa. It may also be because there is a 'high' view of social solidarity and salvation cannot be seen in merely personal terms but must be seen to have social implications. Observers of African churches are often struck by the lack of a division between the churches' social programmes and their evangelistic outreach. This is very unlike the situation in other parts of the world but it has to do with the biblical teaching on wholeness finding a resonance with African values.

The church's struggle through the centuries with the question of slavery is another example of 're-receiving'. The 'household codes' in the New Testament (Ephesians 5:21–6:9; Colossians 3:18–22; 1 Peter 2 and 3) are heavily influenced by the values of the society around the early churches and seem to accept slavery as an institution inherent among human beings. At the same time, such teaching is in tension with central features of New Testament anthropology, such as Galatians 3:28, where we learn that in Christ there is neither male nor female, Jew or Gentile, slave nor free. We find Paul himself struggling with the institution in his letter to Philemon and, we have seen, even in the 'household codes' the dimension of mutuality required in all relationships is a distinctively Christian contribution. We have seen also how slaves enjoyed a status in the church that was very different from their treatment in the world outside. All of this is true, but it has to be admitted that slavery as an institution was not challenged until the eighteenth-century evangelical revival in the United Kingdom, and, later on, in other parts of the world. People reading their Bibles could now see that it was not possible to maintain that all human beings were in the image of God, had been redeemed by Christ and needed to hear this good news, and yet also to have some of them as slaves. It is true that evangelicals were also influenced by Enlightenment values of 'benevolence, happiness and liberty', but what drove them to action was the conviction that they were righting a wrong and thus fulfilling God's will.[22] The movement for the abolition of the slave trade, and later on of slavery itself, was grounded in a re-reception of the fundamental biblical teaching that all human beings are equal in dignity and status before God and should, therefore, have their freedom and dignity respected in human society.

The way in which we have come to understand the poor in the Bible also illustrates how we 're-receive' certain elements already found in the deposit of faith. Since the Second World War there has been increasing attention to the 'poor' in the Bible (the *anawim* in the Old Testament and the *ptochoi* in the New.)

The various liberation theologies, as they have emerged in different parts of the world, have moved our understanding of the poor as objects of compassion to the need for justice for them and further to the poor themselves being the agents of the change God wants to bring about in the world. Inevitably, this has led to reflection on the nature of such a God and to a fresh emphasis on the God who suffers with the poor in order to change their situation. This, in turn, has led to a new theological orientation: language about God's will and purpose is not derived solely from the world as it is but from what it ought to be. God's purpose for the poor is seen as a contrast to their present experience, and this is how God becomes their saviour.[23] There has been considerable exegesis of passages in the Pentateuch, in the Prophets and in the Gospels that speak of the poor, and commentators cannot now neglect this important topic. The Beatitudes (especially in Luke), Mary's Song and Jesus' inaugural sermon at Nazareth, for example, cannot now be just spiritualised away. Several New Testament writers, such as Luke and James, are recognised as having a special concern for the poor. True, in the Bible those who trust in God alone are spoken of as 'the poor', but the literally poor cannot be excluded either. Certainly it is not enough to be poor:

response to God's initiative is also necessary. It is then that they inherit the kingdom of God.[24]

Perhaps the most dramatic and also the most controversial instance of re-reception has been that of the place of women in society and in the church. From both implicit and explicit positions on the inferiority of women, the church has begun to re-read and to re-evaluate its own traditions in the light of the Bible and apostolic Tradition. It has to be acknowledged that much of the impetus for this has come from developments outside the church. The changing role and status of women in many societies has alerted the church to the need for re-examining the Bible's teaching on women and men, to the necessity of distinguishing between what is of primary importance in a biblical anthropology, the effects of sin on relationships between women and men and secondary accretions due to historical and cultural factors. As with liberation theology, the church is being helped in this task by women theologians and scholars. These have not limited themselves to criticisms of the patriarchal cultures in which the books of the Bible and the traditions of the churches have arisen. They have rather begun the painful (but also rewarding) work of reconstructing what the Bible is really saying about women, their place in creation and in the church. One aspect of this has been to highlight the maternal and feminine metaphors used of the different persons of the Holy Trinity.[25]

The admission of women to the ordained ministry in various churches has followed the realisation that the church cannot, on the one hand, preach that both men and women have been made in God's image and that in Christ all barriers between the genders have been broken down and, on the other, deny women a place in the ordained ministry. An inclusive church should be represented by an inclusive ministry. Ordained ministers, however, do not merely represent the church; they represent Christ himself (Matthew 10:40–42; John 20:21; 1 Timothy 4:6; etc.). This representation of Christ in the Christian community and to the world is signified, of course, in the saying of the words of institution at the Lord's Supper or the Eucharist. Some have argued that only a male may properly represent the incarnate Lord. This is, of course, to misunderstand the nature of the Lord's risen and glorified humanity, which includes people of every race and of both genders (Ephesians 2:6). It is fitting, therefore, that the inclusive Christ should be represented by an inclusive ministry.[26]

Apart from the strictly theological arguments, a great deal of work was done during the twentieth century to highlight the role of women in the Bible and the church. This ranges from exercising a ministry of prophecy (2 Kings 22:14–20; Acts 21:9; 1 Corinthians 11:5), of leadership among God's people (Judges 4:4; Acts 16:15; Romans 16:3–5), to mission (Romans 16:3; Philippians 4:2; Romans 16:7) and teaching (Acts 18:26). Whatever else we may say of the place and role of women in the church, it must be in the light of the central affirmations in the Bible regarding women and men and also of the heroic women who have been mentioned in the Bible and in the church's Tradition.

Whatever decisions particular churches may have made regarding the ordination of women, it remains true that their position is changing rapidly in *all* the churches. I was in Rome when the Pope spoke on the eve of the United Nations Conference in Beijing on women. He highlighted the place of women in the received Tradition and then went on to list all the things women could now do in the Roman Catholic Church. These ranged from pastoral work to teaching, to serving and being 'extraordinary ministers' in the distribution of the eucharistic elements. None of these would have been possible only a few years ago.

Orthodox women too, both 'Eastern' and 'Oriental', are busy in reviewing the Tradition and discovering the place of women in it. A recent meeting in Damascus concluded its declaration in this way:

> throughout the history of the church, we have the testimony of countless women saints who responded to Christ in many ways, such as *apostles*, evangelists, confessors, martyrs, ascetics and nuns, teachers, mothers, spiritual and medical healers, and deaconesses. We orthodox women of today, inspired through the prayers and example of these women saints, now endeavour to continue in their footsteps, as we too strive to respond to our Lord's call: 'follow me'. Amen.[27]

The process of reception poses particular difficulties because of division among the churches. A family of churches, for example, may come to a mind that it is right to ordain women, but that may immediately jeopardise their conversations about greater unity with churches that have decided it is *not* right to do so. This is the case with the dialogues between the Anglican communion, on the one hand, and the Roman Catholic, Orthodox and ancient oriental churches on the other. In spite of landmark agreements on the nature of salvation, the church, the Eucharist and the ministry, unity still seems far away because of a new difficulty: the ordination of women to the priesthood and, in some provinces, to the episcopate in the Anglican communion. In addition, even when a church comes to a mind on a matter, through its decision-making processes, often a minority remains unconvinced and dissatisfied with the decision. This is the case, for example, with some Anglicans in provinces where women have been ordained. They may have a rigorist position that orders cannot be conferred on women or, while not being 'impossibilists', they may believe that the Anglican communion should not 'go it alone' but should attempt a consensus with the major churches in the world before 're-receiving' the Tradition in this way.

Because of these problems it is increasingly emphasised that reception of new understandings, developments and practices is a continuous process in the church and that the process may result in the new not being received as an authentic expression of the great Tradition, but as a departure from it. In a divided situation it is important that the ecumenical dimensions of the process be recognised.

Yet it is part of the church's missionary task to engage with the world, in all its diversity and dynamism. Out of such engagement may well emerge a new awareness of some aspect of the faith. Such an awareness will have to be received and lived by the whole church as an authentic expression of the faith in this or that situation.[28]

Tradition and development

The receiving of Tradition in a particular context is never merely a repetition of the old. Something new emerges in terms of interpretation, understanding and knowledge when the living Tradition is brought into dialogue with developments in the sciences, the social sciences or literature and art. For some years now I have been a member of the Human Fertilisation and Embryology Authority (HFEA) and chair of its Ethics Committee. The Authority has been set up by Parliament to regulate treatment and research in the field of assisted reproduction. Membership has shown me the extent of knowledge now available to us in terms of the very beginnings of human life, but this has also raised all sorts of questions about personhood and when this can be attributed to the embryo or foetus. Christian Tradition, going back to St Thomas Aquinas, has held that personhood begins with the 'ensoulment' of the foetus, that is to say, the emergence of an organisational and directional principle. For Aquinas, this happens approximately forty days after fertilisation. Interestingly, this is in accord with the scientific view that brain activity commences at about this time. What status has the embryo, then, if it is not yet a full human person? Should it be respected as potentially a human person? Should research be permitted on embryos? And what about 'spare' embryos produced during the course of *in vitro* fertilisation – how should they be treated? Can a process that produces such embryos be permissible? It will be obvious that such debate is bringing about an understanding of the human person that takes account of developments in science but is also continuous with the Tradition. The interaction has produced something new, yet organically related to the old. It is not, then, just a question of reception but of *development* in the church's understanding of Tradition and how it relates to contemporary knowledge.

The problem about development, drawing out the implications of Tradition in the light of scientific and other discoveries, is that it could become unprincipled. If such development is possible, people will want to justify their pet theories and even prejudices in this way. That is why we need *criteria* to discern what is authentic development from Tradition. For John Henry Newman the notes of genuine development had to do with the preservation and vigour of the original idea, continuity of principles and anticipation of the future, a conservative way of allowing development from Tradition.[29]

We may say that authentic development will come from genuine *engagement* with the world around us. If I am ever to make a contribution to a Christian view of the human person in the twenty-first century, it will be because I am associated with the HFEA. I have found that such bodies welcome a Christian presence. This does not automatically mean agreement with what Christians wish to commend, as the world is a market place and Christians need to argue their case as much as anyone else. No view has a privileged position and there is no place for laziness.

Secondly, development must be *organically* related to the Tradition. While the imaginative reception and expression of Tradition has always been vital, such imagination cannot be cut loose from its moorings. I am not talking about sharp discontinuities and radically new insights, but of continuous progress in understanding, even if, from time to time, the church has to be called back to basics.

Thirdly, development must make it easier for our contemporaries to hear and to understand the good news of God's saving intention and work. It must, at once, clarify both the deposit of faith and the contemporary situation. It must help people to resolve problems of belief and of behaviour. It should enable the church both to preach and to live the gospel more *effectively.*

If the church is shaped not only by the world in which it finds itself but also by its inner dynamic, Tradition, which is itself shaped by Scripture and the continuing work of the Holy Spirit, will appear in certain ways which may be regarded as fundamental. At the same time, the church is a mystery (Ephesians 5:32) and we cannot understand everything about it all at once. This is why 'modelling' different aspects of the church is necessary. People are discovering new ways of being 'church' and this raises many important questions for the future. It is to these issues that we now move.

3. Fundamentals of Being Church

CASE STUDY

Jez and Penny live on an upmarket estate in the south-east of England. It is beautifully planned and the only thing it lacks is a church! They offer their house as a place where local Christians can meet and the Church of England offers a priest, part-time, to lead their worship and mission in the community. Soon they are holding services in the school hall. The headmistress is very co-operative and the buildings are spanking new. Groups continue, however, to meet in Jez and Penny's home. In the meantime, the parishes, of which the estate is formally a part, are beginning to get interested in what is going on.

How should the church in Jez and Penny's home continue to operate? Should there be other 'house churches' around the estate? How often should they all meet together in the school? What is their relation to the 'mother parishes'? Where will the 'occasional offices', baptisms, weddings and funerals, be held – on the estate or in the historic churches? How should the diocese, as well as the other denominations, contribute to the mission of the church on the estate? Are there fundamental ways of 'being church' that cannot be ignored?

Because the world is as it is and because the church lives a faith that stays the same throughout the ages and all over the world, the church appears in certain 'shapes' that are fundamental to its nature, which we may regard as 'norms'. This in no way denies that these shapes may themselves be affected by varying situations and needs. Indeed, we shall see that this *is* the case in many parts of the world and should be the case everywhere!

It seems that in the New Testament period there were three, or perhaps four, basic categories of the church. There was, first of all, *the church in people's homes*, or perhaps we should say the *household* as church. This would have included the extended family as well as servants and slaves. It seems, however, that it was more than that. The greetings in the letters to the house churches imply a wider gathering than just the family, and we know that, in some cases at least, the large upper room was used as a place of meeting (Acts 2:46; 20:7f; Romans 16:5, 14–15; 1 Corinthians 16:19; Colossians 4:15; Philemon 2; etc.). Prisca (or Priscilla) and Aquila and the church in their house are mentioned more than once. It is thought that Prisca is often mentioned first by both Luke in the Acts of the Apostles and by Paul because she was the leader in 'her family', whether because of her impressive personality, her social standing, hospitality or gift of teaching.[1] She is not, though, the only woman leader of this kind. Lydia (Acts 16:14f), Chloe (1 Corinthians 1:11) and Nympha (Colossians 4:15) are also such leaders of churches. Their leadership in a household church raises all sorts of questions about what is said regarding 'headship' of the male in other parts of the New Testament (1 Corinthians 11:3; 1 Timothy 2:12). Is headship a formal principle inherited by Paul from the Judaism of his day and his observation of the gentile world all around, which is, nevertheless, cracking open under pressure from the egalitarianism of the gospel Paul himself preaches and also the charismatic gifts being exercised by women leaders? It is held sometimes that headship has to do with the family, not the church. Here too, however, the principle of mutuality, a prominent feature of Pauline teaching, places strict restrictions on any surviving notion of such headship (Ephesians 5:21).

The church in people's homes was certainly important for worship – in fact, even on the Lord's Day worship is mentioned in the New Testament as taking place in a home. Homes were important also for teaching. Note how Prisca and Aquila 'take' Apollos to their home and explain, more accurately, the way of God to him (Acts 18:26). From 1 Corinthians and elsewhere, we know that Apollos was to become a great leader of the church – someone who could be mentioned in the same breath as Paul himself!

Those working in the sociology of the New Testament tell us that, alongside full-time missionaries and catechists, the witness in and of the Christian home was crucial for the spreading of the good news throughout the ancient world. This may have been the witness of a Christian wife to her husband, of a slave to his or her owners, or of hosts to guests (hospitality was greatly emphasised in the early church: e.g. Romans 12:13; Hebrews 13:2).[2]

The second church category is that of *the church in a particular locality*: the people of God from a town or a village gathering together to eat, to worship and to discuss matters of significance for them. In Asia this would have been generally in the upper room of a house, but in Rome they would have needed another part of the house. Eventually, of course, many of these houses were adapted, particularly when the congregation had grown rapidly in size. Some were, indeed, donated for the sole use of the congregation and, from the third century at the latest, there is evidence of specific buildings being erected for use as churches. Christians sometimes gathered out of doors and, on the anniversaries of martyrs and at time of persecution, in the catacombs where the martyrs were buried. Acts 19:9 may be an indication that at times Christians were willing to rent or borrow buildings for their own use.[3] It is also true, of course, that the earliest Christians gathered in the Temple at Jerusalem (Acts 2:46), attended synagogues and frequented less formal 'places of prayer' (Acts 16:16).

As we have seen, people *did* gather to break bread in homes but, more characteristically, the Eucharist was celebrated when Christians from all over the town or a locality gathered together. The account in 1 Corinthians 11 is of such a celebration (see particularly vv. 20–22). This meeting, a common assembly for the breaking of bread and, from time to time, for the baptism of new converts, is mentioned and commended by the earliest Christian writers, such as Ignatius of Antioch (martyred about AD 110) and Justin Martyr (martyred about AD 165).[4]

At a time when barriers were being broken down between people of different religious, ethnic and social groups, this wider gathering was significant for the unity of the church. If churches in people's *homes* nurtured believers in the faith among those only with whom they felt comfortable, the gathering of the *whole church* in Corinth, Ephesus or Troas was a challenge to meet with all who were members of the body of Christ. The capacity of the early church both to break down barriers and to give people a sense of their inalienable dignity, whatever their standing in the world outside, can be identified as one of the leading causes for the rapid spread of the church throughout the ancient world.[5]

Already in the New Testament groups of such local churches also came to be seen as having a particular relationship of mutual support and, sometimes, of a challenge to faithfulness. In his letter to the Colossians (4:16) St Paul is aware of such a relationship between the church in Colosse and the one in Laodicea. Peter's first letter is addressed to the churches in Western Asia and John the Divine's Revelation to the seven churches of Asia. The last two would have been carried from church to church and this presupposes communication among these churches, as well as common problems and opportunities.[6]

In the second century bishops of different local churches in an area met together, particularly at times of crisis and, in the East, this led to the organisation of the church into *provinces* along the lines of the political provinces in the Roman Empire. The bishop of the leading city in the area became a kind of *primus inter pares* (a 'first among equals'). This involved him in leadership in the task of electing new bishops in his area and also in certain matters of discipline as well as of relationships with churches outside the region. For obvious reasons such a bishop came to be called a 'metropolitan' (known sometimes in the West as 'archbishop'). In the West, provinces developed neither so clearly nor so rapidly (though they *did* emerge). Rome in Europe and Carthage in North Africa were the dominant sees and, from time to time, there was conflict between them. Cyprian, who was Bishop of Carthage in the third century, both acknowledged the pre-eminence of the see of Rome as the *cathedra Petri* (the 'chair of Peter') and claimed due autonomy for his African province in matters of appointment and discipline. He was also not afraid to criticise the Roman church and its bishop when he believed them to be in opposition to the church's Tradition and to 'truth' as he saw it. We know that in holding such opinions he was not alone.[7] It is interesting to note that in the North African province, the bishops met together with clergy and laity and the bishops consulted the clergy and laity before making important decisions in the life of the church. At the same time, Cyprian was very aware of the authority he had received as a bishop and of the responsibility this involved.

The emergence of 'national' churches both in the Orthodox world and, at the time of the Reformation, in Western Europe, is an expression of the 'provincial' idea, although it had also to do, of course, with the emergence of nation-states at different times in history.

We have noted how the New Testament term for 'church' is used of households and the gatherings connected with these. It is used also of local churches in particular towns or cities. We have seen, moreover, that these churches are not regarded as isolated entities but as mutually interrelated and interdependent. They have a care not only for one another's spiritual needs but also for their material needs (Acts 11:27–30; Romans 15:25–28; 1 Corinthians 16:1–4; 2 Corinthians 8 and 9). It is not surprising, therefore, to discover that already in the later New Testament a strong sense of the universal church is emerging, the body of Christ of which he is the Head (e.g. Ephesians 1:22; 2:21; 3:10, 21; 5:32; Colossians 1:18, 24; etc.).

The term 'catholic', meaning 'general' or 'universal', is first used by Ignatius of Antioch. In his letter to the Christians of Smyrna he tells them, 'Where Christ Jesus is, there is the catholic church.' In time, 'catholic' came to mean not only the church throughout the world, but also down the ages. This last idea is expressed in the Apostles' Creed as 'the communion of saints'. The sharing of all Christians in 'holy things', such as a common worship of God and participation in the sacraments, leads to a close fellowship among them. Nor is such a fellowship confined to the church on earth at any one time. The prayers of the saints on earth are received along with the worship of the saints in heaven (Revelation 7:9 – 8:5). The church continues to give glory to Christ throughout all generations. Even in heaven it is to proclaim the manifold wisdom of God (Ephesians 3:10, 21). At the Lord's Supper we join the angels, archangels and 'all the company of heaven' in praising God.

'Catholic' came to be used not only of the universal church but also of its faith: 'what is believed everywhere, always and by all'. This is the so-called canon of faith of St Vincent of Lérins (died c. AD 450). In this sense it is used to describe the continuous tradition of faith and practice that, in spite of local variations, has its origins in the Scriptures and in the faith and practice of the apostles. It is one of the ways in which the true church of Jesus Christ is 'marked out'.

The basis of membership of this church is, of course, faith in Christ and baptism by water in the name of the Trinity. This implies that people will be members of particular churches as well. Even so, the limits of the universal church cannot be defined simply with reference to the local churches. There may well be 'secret believers', those who have received the 'baptism of desire' but not of water, and those whose institutional links with the local church are tenuous at best. In a divided situation, moreover, we are beginning to recognise that our common baptism in the faith is the basis of our unity in Christ. Once this is recognised, however, we must also go on to recognise that the church of Jesus Christ is present wherever and whenever Christians gather together. The extent and the modes of this presence may be matters for discussion, but its reality cannot be denied. Recognition of this presence is itself a way of promoting unity, as is a common submission to God's word and the giving and receiving of spiritual riches that various traditions have preserved and nurtured.

This cannot be all, however. The universal church is 'represented' or 'embodied' in the *local* churches (1 Corinthians 1:2), just as it is 'made up' of *all* the particular churches. There is a relationship of mutuality here for which explanations of the universal church as an invisible body, whose actual membership is known only to God, are simply inadequate. As for local churches, we also need structures in the universal church that allow for meeting one another, for encouragement and support. From time to time there may be a need to exercise discipline, and sometimes it may be necessary to discuss matters of faith and practice and to set the boundaries of permissible diversity. Local and national churches have such structures and mechanisms (perhaps 'organs' is a better word) and there is every reason why the worldwide church should also have them.

The universality of the church's calling is already given at the time of Pentecost when different people are drawn to its message and the church speaks in a language all can understand (Acts 2:1–11). This sense of the church's already present, yet coming, universality pervades the earliest Christian writings. Ignatius is aware of it at the beginning of the second century. Irenaeus towards its end and Clement of Alexandria at the beginning of the third.[8] Sometimes when a local church has become overidentified with a nation, a people or a culture, it has forgotten about this universality and this sense of a universal mission. But the church as a whole has never forgotten it and, from time to time, one part of the church can remind another of this important aspect of the Christian faith. When, for example, the churches of the Reformation were sunk deep in their overidentification with the emergent European state, the Counter-Reformation in the Roman Catholic Church, with its missionary zeal, stood as a witness against them on this account. In the same way, many Anglican and Protestant missionary efforts in the nineteenth century aimed, first of all, to reawaken the missionary impulse in the ancient churches of the Middle East, Asia and Africa.[9] Today it is, perhaps, the turn of vibrant churches in Africa, Latin America and Asia to renew the missionary vision of churches in Europe and other parts of the 'West'.

It is important to note that making decisions together and being missionary together should take place in the context of *habitual* giving and receiving. Every church has something to offer: it may be a firmness of faith, eagerness to share it, gifts of the Spirit, riches of devotion and scholarship or material goods. In the same way, every church needs to receive from the others: whether this is in terms of courageous witness, spontaneity in worship, seriousness of study or transparency in handling the church's material and spiritual resources.

As in the local church, so also in the worldwide church, the celebration of the Eucharist both demonstrates Christian unity and is a means of achieving it. From time to time it is possible to make visible the eucharistic unity of the worldwide church in a dramatic way. In an Anglican context, for instance, the Lambeth Conference of Bishops can be such an occasion. The unity can, however, be shown in other, less dramatic, ways. For example, by praying for the world church and its leaders at a local Eucharist, by having ministers officiate who are recognised as those authorised to do so by churches throughout the world, by the use of music and other means of devotion from different parts of the world. As always, the difficulty of churches divided among themselves presents itself. How much agreement in faith should there be before Christians from different traditions can take part together in the Lord's Supper?

Should the presidents at such celebrations be those who are acknowledged as standing in a certain relationship with the church worldwide and down the ages? Should there be agreement about the meaning of what we are doing?

Some Christians hold that, in spite of differences on these matters, we should celebrate the Eucharist together and participate in one another's celebrations as a way of building our unity. They point out that it is the *Lord's* Supper and not ours. We should let him be the judge of what we and others believe about his body and blood. In any case, too much blood has been spilt over these matters. We should simply trust the Lord's promise and take what he gives. Such people sometimes remind others of Elizabeth I and her eirenic saying:

> 'Twas God the Word that spake it:
> He took the Bread and brake it:
> And what the Word did make it
> That I believe and take it.

Charity must, however, have limits and we know that in the early church there was an elaborate system of determining whether someone should be admitted to table fellowship as, indeed, there still is in certain kinds of free churches and, of course, in the Roman Catholic and Orthodox churches. The certificates, letters and commendations of the early period allowed the host congregation to determine the good standing of a person in their previous church and whether they shared the faith of the hosts. Anglicans, for example, offer eucharistic hospitality to members of other Christian churches, but this is on the basis that we share the same faith and have at least some elements in common as far as eucharistic faith is concerned. In the same way, if Anglicans are offered hospitality elsewhere they may decide to receive communion on the basis that, because of our common baptism, elements of Christ's church are present, even if other elements, such as continuity of ministry down the ages as Anglicans understand it, are not.

The problem is more acute when church leaders are present at an official occasion when it is more difficult to go against the rules of one's own church. One solution sometimes adopted is that of joint presidency on such occasions.[10]

Again, however, this demands at least minimal agreement about the nature of the sacrament. All of this goes to show that, in a divided church, there are no easy answers to eucharistic sharing. At the same time, we need to acknowledge that the Eucharist can be a means of building Christian unity and some anomalies must, therefore, be tolerated. They should not, however, be multiplied beyond necessity.

If there are fundamental ways in which the church must show itself, then these will have significance for us today. In the 1970s and 1980s there was a general sense that the home as the locus of the church should be re-emphasised. In many of the mainstream churches there was great flowering of home groups that met for worship, Bible study and fellowship. Some, however, began to hold that the 'house church' was the *only* legitimate manifestation of the church. They were disillusioned with the historic denominations and felt that God was beginning a new work through the emergent house churches. Many of them grew so quickly, however, that the term 'house' had to be extended to cover cinema, school hall and even purpose-built premises!

With the historic churches, on the other hand, there is a growing realisation that house groups can become closed and inward-looking. There is a need to make them more missionary-minded as well as more supportive of existing members. At the same time, the importance of the local church is being recognised afresh. It is here that people with different backgrounds come together. It is a place for teaching and building up the body of Christ. From here Christians can make an impact on the wider community, whether in terms of partnership or of prophetic challenge. In Western Europe, at any rate, the nation-state is assuming a lower profile and there is both growth of regionalism and of European identity. This may mean that the 'provincial idea' becomes more important. Groups of churches in particular regions may often be the way in which the gospel is heard in civil society. At the same time, churches are increasingly conscious of their European-wide role: making sure that developing institutions and laws continue to reflect Christian values and lead to as open and inclusive a Europe as is possible in today's world. Again, in a situation where Christians are, according to the US State Department, the most persecuted people in the world, the universal church as manifested in a fellowship of local churches is a most important network for mutual prayer and support. Also, as Christians try to address prophetically the big issues of sharing resources, caring for the environment and defending the weak, it is crucial that they are seen as a worldwide movement.

4. Models of the Church

We have seen that the essential features of the church continue to have relevance in our own times. The church is, however, a *mystery*. I do not mean by this the 'mystification' that can surround our language, worship or ways of doing things. Where this exists, we should, of course, try to remove it so that people can encounter the living God in our witnessing and worshipping. No, I mean that it is a mystery in the theological sense regarding the church's relation to Christ (Ephesians 5:32). Such a relationship is both revealed and hidden. However much is said about it, something remains unsaid and, perhaps, it is something that cannot be said. This is one reason why people often speak of 'models of the church'. In science, for instance, modelling is used when a particular aspect of reality cannot be fully understood. Models are then developed to highlight different features of what is being studied. Similarly, since we cannot immediately understand everything about the church, we need models that will highlight for us one aspect or another as needs in mission and pastoral work require. I cannot, of course, give you *all* the models or metaphors that have ever been used, but we shall look at some of the main ones found in the Bible itself that have been used extensively in the course of Christian history. The models are not, of course, mutually exclusive. They are complementary and more than one can be used at any one time to further our understanding of the church's nature and purpose. Each of them, moreover, has its own strengths and weaknesses that also need acknowledgement and reflection.

The church as body

There is, then, first of all, the *organic* model: language about the church as the body of Christ is rooted in the New Testament itself. In both the letter to the Romans (ch. 12) and the first letter to the Christians at Corinth (ch. 12 again), St Paul speaks of the church, in its different manifestations, as the body of Christ. It seems that this image or model was especially significant for Paul for a number of reasons. It is thought, for example, that his experience of the risen Lord identifying himself with his people ('I am Jesus whom you are persecuting'), at the time of Paul's conversion, never left him and he continued to think of the church as somehow a manifestation of Christ himself. Again, it is said, that his experience of the Eucharist showed him that those who partake of the one bread are, indeed, one body (1 Corinthians 10:17).[1]

This model of the church as 'body' was greatly developed in patristic and mediaeval times. Indeed, in some periods of church history, it became the ruling paradigm of the church. As the church became more acceptable in the Roman Empire and went on to become the guarantor of social order, in West and East, it became natural to speak of both the church and the wider civil society as a hierarchically ordered body. In the West, in particular, and until very recently in the Roman Catholic Church, the institutional aspect of the church was identified absolutely with the mystical body of Christ. Only the Second Vatican Council refused to make this identification in such absolute terms.[2]

In the Church of England, also, the body metaphor has been extensively used in the course of institutional reform.[3] Once again, the church as the body of Christ has been closely identified with the institutional structures and arrangements of one particular church.

The strengths of this model are that we are talking about close interdependence between the parts or members of the body. Each member has been given particular gifts for the sake of the whole body and all have a duty to care for one another and to nurture the gifts that each has been given. The difficulty with the body metaphor has sometimes been that it is perceived as too static. Each member or part has its appointed place and this can be used to justify a rigidly hierarchical church and a 'bless the squire and his relations' view of wider society. It is also claimed sometimes that the body model is strongly assimilative and does not leave room for dissent and for the individual conscience. It can be used to justify an already existing institutional structure in church or society or to promote a structure that some would like to see.

In addition to the body language discussed above, another kind of metaphor occurs in the New Testament and is used in subsequent writing. This is the one we find in the letters to the Colossians and the Ephesians. Here it is a matter not merely of body but of body *and head*: *Caput et Membra* (Ephesians 4:15–16; Colossians 1:18). Christ is the head of the body, and the whole body is ordered towards him and derives its coherence from him. The New Testament letters do not ask explicitly how the head is represented in and for the body, even if Pope Pius XII was clear in his famous encyclical that it is the bishops and clergy who are the 'joints and ligaments' mentioned in Ephesians, and everything else that remains is the faithful![4] Once again, the Second Vatican Council corrected this tendency by teaching, in its document on the laity, that all the baptised have an apostolic calling.[5]

The language of priesthood used of the whole church shows clearly that all believers represent and proclaim Christ in the world (1 Peter 2:9). The whole church can act with authority because of Christ's presence within it (Matthew 18:15–21). All can, through Christ, offer the sacrifice of praise (Hebrews 13:15). Even individual believers witness to Christ when they confess his name (particularly when the environment is hostile) and when they bring God's renewal to the world (e.g. John 7:38; Romans 10:9–21). Such witness was particularly crucial in the early years of the faith. When family members saw how the Christian faith had changed their relatives, they could not help being influenced by it. When even slaves and young children bore fearless witness in the courts and, sometimes, went fearlessly to torture and certain death, they were a way of bringing Christ to the world. Today also in many parts of the world where Christians are suffering, such courageous testimony is being given.

CASE STUDY

The blind evangelist Mehdi Dibaj told the Clerical Court in Iran, which was to sentence him to death, how Christ's transforming love had changed him to such an extent that he could not only pray for his persecutors but love them! Bernard Levin was so impressed with Mehdi's witness that he devoted a whole article in The Times *to it. Mehdi was freed after international pressure had been brought to bear, but a short time later was murdered as he walked in a park.*

And yet the New Testament and later Christianity is full of examples which show us that Christian ministers represent Christ and God the Father, in both church and world, in a distinctive way. Along with the rest of God's covenant people, they share in the royal priesthood of Christ, but they also speak and act for Christ in a way that is different. We may not all want to endorse the Anglican–Roman Catholic International Commission's Report when it speaks of ministerial priesthood as belonging to 'another realm' in its representational role.[6] Distinctiveness, nevertheless, has to be recognised. In his sending out of the Twelve, Jesus is quite clear when he says, 'He who receives you receives me, and he who receives me receives the one who sent me' (Matthew 10:40). It is clear that such a representational role has to do with the authority received from Jesus, though St Luke also reminds us that such representative authority must be exercised with great humility (9:48). All the Gospels end with a commissioning of the disciples to continue the mission of Jesus (it is significant that both the so-called shorter and longer endings of Mark's Gospel have this missionary element), and the Acts of the Apostles begin with such a charge. Even if the wider circle of disciples is seen as present on some of these occasions, it is clear that the apostles have a special position in relation to the rest.

This awareness of a special kind of authority to represent Christ is also found in the writings of St Paul. The second letter to the Corinthians is a good example: in chapter 3, for instance, Paul is speaking clearly along with the believers. 'All of us', he says, 'go on from one kind of glory to another' (2 Corinthians 3:18, my translation). In the very next verse, however, which begins the new chapter (though Paul did not of course divide his letter into chapters and verses!), he changes tack and begins to speak of the particular ministry, the apostolic ministry, he had received. The next few chapters can only be understood if this is borne in mind.[7] Augustine of Hippo, perhaps from his reading of St Paul, sums up the tension of this dual reality in his famous saying *Vobis enim sum episcopus, vobiscum sum Christianus* ('for you I am a bishop, with you I am a Christian'). In preaching the word, in presiding at the celebration of the sacraments (particularly in baptising people in the name of the blessed Trinity and in reciting the words of the institution at the Lord's Supper) and in being representative figures within the church and for the world, Christian ministers exercise a special ministry that is not just about the ministry of all the baptised. It is not even a ministry of representing the church. It has to do with representing Christ in a way that is different from other kinds of representation. Because of this, such ministry cannot be understood in merely functional terms but must be seen as a 'charism' or gift given in the calling, preparing and ordering of such ministers. Such a gift needs constant nurture and renewal if ordained ministry is to be effective (2 Timothy 1:6–7).

Even if we do not take Pius XII's use of Ephesians to justify the institutional arrangements in the Roman Catholic Church too seriously, we can agree that a 'head and body' type of ecclesiology has some roots in the New Testament. It is also true, however, that such an understanding of the church can lead to even more abuses than the more general 'body' language. It can be used to create a hierarchical structure with a clerical caste at its apex. It can be used to privilege such a caste and it can be used to neglect the role of lay people in consultation and decision-making. It is, however, necessary for order in the church, for clear leadership and for appropriate co-ordination in the community at local, regional and universal levels. Such an understanding should not be allowed to become the only way of thinking about the church but must be complemented by other more egalitarian and dynamic models.

One danger of the 'body of Christ' model that has often been pointed out is that it tends to 'divinise' the church. This can have two interrelated results: it heightens the role of church as *the* agent for bringing about the kingdom of God and this can seem to restrict divine sovereignty and God's freedom to act as he chooses. On the other hand, it makes it more difficult to think of the church as weak and sinful and even in error. This has the result of making reform more problematic. If the church is truly *ecclesia semper reformanda* ('an ever-reforming body'), that must imply that it is human and fallible, needing constantly to submit to God's word, to repent and to change.

The church as communion or fellowship

Language about the church as *koinonia* or communion has sprung into prominence largely because of ecumenical work that commends this way of understanding the church as more conducive to the promotion of Christian unity. The point of departure for such thinking is often the life of the blessed Trinity itself and the intensely intimate relations among the three persons of the one God. There is a sense, of course, in which these relations are unique. The doctrine of *perichoresis* tells us that the persons are in such a close union that the thought, love and action of each can also be regarded as those of the others. Human beings do not have any experience of such a close unity and we need to be careful in speaking of the unity of the church in terms drawn directly from trinitarian theology.

Scripture does, however, speak of the church's unity as related to that of the Holy Trinity and this evidence cannot, therefore, be neglected. The farewell discourses in St John's Gospel have been a fertile source for thinking about the relationship between the Trinity and the church: just as Jesus is in the Father and the Father is in him, so also the disciples are in Jesus and Jesus is in the disciples (14:10, 20). The Spirit is also spoken of as 'in' or 'among' the disciples (14:17) while Paul tells us in Galatians what 'life in the Spirit' should look like (5:22–25). In his High Priestly prayer, also, Jesus asks that the unity of the church may be like the mutual indwelling of the Father and the Son.

The strongly incorporationist tone of the New Testament makes it clear that our communion with the Godhead is based on our baptism into Christ (Romans 6:1–11) and our participation in the Eucharist (1 Corinthians 10:14–22). It is based on the work of the Holy Spirit who leads us to call God 'Abba' (Romans 8:15). It is in our receiving of the divine promises that we become partakers of the divine nature (2 Peter 1:4).

It is because of our fellowship with God that we can have fellowship with one another (1 John 1:3). The churches are increasingly recognising that all Christians, whatever their differences, are in a state of real communion with one another because of their common baptism. It is also true, of course, that what has been given in baptism needs to be realised in the daily living of Christians and churches. Indeed, the fellowship brought about by baptism into Christ impels us towards greater unity.[8]

The communion model is increasingly popular because, at the local level, it recognises the interpersonal nature of belonging to a fellowship and, at other levels, it gives us the means to deal creatively with diversity. Of course, this cannot be mere diversity, as that would not lead to unity but only to greater chaos. It must be legitimate diversity, recognised by all as such. Such diversity may exist because of cultural and linguistic factors or it may be due to different church traditions. The Orthodox churches, for example, are all in communion with one another even though their cultural situation can vary enormously. In the same way, the Roman Catholic Church recognises that the oriental churches in communion with it have very different liturgical and disciplinary traditions. Pope Paul VI recognised that the 'patrimony' of the Anglican communion – its spiritual and liturgical heritage – would have to be respected if there was to be greater unity between Anglicans and Roman

Catholics.[9] Similarly, any advance in Anglican–Methodist unity should respect the missionary background and structure of the Methodist movement.[10]

The communion model plays down the importance of a visible structure as a sign and guarantor of unity. It emphasises interpersonal encounter and diversity in unity rather than the somewhat inflexible unity of a single organisation that the 'body' image can be seen to demand. As the Orthodox theologian John Zizioulas has pointed out, it is in the fellowship of a particular church and in the fellowship among particular churches that the apostolic faith is received, lived and handed on.[11] The ordained ministry, when it is faithful, is indeed an effective sign, a sign going back to the beginnings of the church, of such unity. It is, however, the whole church that is apostolic in faith and witness. In extreme circumstances, a church may, for various reasons, lose this sign and yet retain its apostolicity, even if it needs to restore the sign when it has become possible to do so.[12]

There *is* a tendency, though, for people to use this model to 'spiritualise' the unity of Christians in an ideal and mystical way and to avoid the hard work of making such unity visible for the sake of the church's mission in the world. Again, in spite of its antipathy to the institutional, this model can be used to exclude those with whom we do not agree. It is true, of course, that fellowship depends on *some* agreement about essentials, but the intention should be to include people as much as possible, rather than to exclude. The Roman Catholic Church, for instance, recognises that it is in a real, though imperfect, communion with all who have been baptised in the name of the Trinity, but it has been slow to acknowledge the ecclesial implications of such a view, even if the Second Vatican Council, and various popes, have been willing to say that the true church of Christ is present in various ecclesial bodies to the extent that they have retained catholic faith and order.[13] Recognition of common baptism has also not led to a greater sharing in the Eucharist, as a way of building up the unity of the church, at least with Anglicans and Protestants. Consciousness of our *common* baptism should lead to a *common* confession of faith, a *common* sacramental life and a *common* mission in the world. In the meantime, there can be many stages in our recognition of one another's discipleship.

The communion model is also interpreted juridically as far as the internal discipline of the Roman Catholic Church is concerned. Theologians are finding, for example, that they have to subscribe to very institutional ways of understanding communion, if they are to retain their good standing. Whether unity in reconciled diversity ever becomes possible depends largely on churches being seen to encourage legitimate diversity within the present denominational structures, as well as recognising it across them.

The pilgrim people of God

We live in a fast-moving world where people are highly mobile. In such a world we need a dynamic model of the church. The noted sociologist of religion, Dr Grace Davie, has referred to those, like the late Princess of Wales, who think of themselves as seekers and pilgrims travelling towards a greater knowledge of truth and a greater experience of love. This is a major trend in people's spirituality today and must not be neglected when we speak of the church.

Once again, the Second Vatican Council has given us the vocabulary we need. While it uses both 'body' and 'communion' language, its preferred model is that of *the pilgrim people of God*.[14] Such language is rooted in the Bible. The Older Testament, in its account of the Exodus from Egypt, speaks of the pilgrim people of God, and the New Testament echoes this language (e.g. in 1 Peter). 'People of God' terminology has wide appeal in a world where popular democracy is recognised as an ideal and 'pilgrim people' has resonances because of its dynamism and because people feel that they are travelling towards a goal rather than a sense that they have attained it. In a highly institutionalised context, it was a way of saying that the institution, however venerable and necessary, is not final. Even if people have assurance of God's love and care in the here and now, they are also pressing on to something that has not been attained and may not even be clearly seen (Philippians 3:12; 1 Corinthians 13:12). In such a dynamic and fluid situation, movements of mission, of prayer, of communal living, can be highly creative in building up the church's pilgrim nature and also its unity.

Such an understanding of the church may also lead us to re-reading its history. This would not then be seen as the development of the institution and the struggles of the hierarchy in obtaining compliance. It would be seen much more as a history of movements – the monastic movement, for example, which challenged Caesaro-papism in the East, and in the West saved Europe from being wholly engulfed by the barbarian invasions and the Dark Ages. It would be seen in movements of pilgrimage to the Holy Land, to Santiago de Compostella and even to Canterbury! The great missionary movements of the Counter-Reformation and of the eighteenth- and nineteenth-century Evangelical Revival would merit more attention than the vicissitudes of the papacy or the complacency of Church of England bishops during this period. The movements of large numbers of 'untouchables' to Christian faith in India and Africa as the new 'Christian continent' would assume a fresh significance. Popular movements within the churches in the Two-Thirds world, which are committed to promoting greater community with the poor, empowerment for the powerless, justice for the oppressed and new ways of being church, would come to the centre of our attention.

The institutional church would, then, encourage voluntary movements of different kinds so that Christian life may be enriched. There is a great deal to be said for this model, but like all the others it has weaknesses as well. For instance, it appears to be arrogant. It limits the term 'the people of God' to those in the churches and the question is asked, 'Are not all people "the people of God" in some sense?' God has created them, has a purpose for them and wants them to be saved. Why single out just the church in this way? This is not, of course, an entirely new question. My Palestinian friends often raise it in relation to Israel: Why one people when there are so many? As we have remarked already, God's choice of Israel, his choice, indeed, of Christ himself and his choice of the church is for the fulfilment of his universal purposes. As Jesus has shown so clearly in his living and dying, election is not for privilege but for proclamation and service. Thus if the church is referred to as 'the people of

God', it is so that *all* may be the people of God. The church is not only a sign and a foretaste of this but also a means of bringing it about. The pilgrim people are also a missionary people.

A learning and witnessing community

Being disciples is basic to being Christian. As we sit under God's word (read, preached and celebrated in the sacraments), we are all learners. We learn also from one another and from God's world. We learn from the past and for the future. It is true that loving never ends; neither does learning!

Within this learning community there are those who have been given special responsibility to make sure that the give and take of mutual learning goes on. They also have a particular task in preaching and teaching (1 Timothy 4:13; 5:17). In all the lists of the different ministries in the church, the ministry of teachers is invariably mentioned (Romans 12:7; 1 Corinthians 12:28; Ephesians 4:11). It seems also that this ministry was especially related to presiding in the community. Such a ministry particularly needs authorisation and proper credentials so that it may be accountable to the church as well as to God (James 3:1).

The proclamation of the word in preaching and in the sacraments is particularly for the building up of those who have already been drawn into the household of faith, but the church also has the role of *herald* to the world. This model has a strong evangelistic thrust to it. People need to hear the good news because their lives and relationships can be changed by it. This, in turn, should usher in a transformed social order and a better world. The proclamation of the gospel is essential because it declares that we become truly human only as we respond to God's love. We begin to discover, then, what makes for our well-being and for that of the world around us. Again, it is the task of the whole community to witness to God's saving acts. As Bishop Lesslie Newbigin put it, the congregation is the truest and most effective hermeneutic of the gospel.[15] Nevertheless the New Testament knows of those who are called to be evangelists (e.g. Acts 21:8; Ephesians 4:11). Even if this title is not used much in the history of the church, there are apostolic men and women who go out to proclaim, to baptise and to nurture. Evangelists are people with particular gifts who can share the gospel effectively. This may be either locally or on the wider stage; it may be with small groups or in mass meetings.

In the Diocese of Rochester, we have been able to revive an order of parish-based evangelists. The inspiration for this came from a visit of some of our clergy to the church in Uganda but, of course, the selection, training and deployment of these evangelists takes place in the light of our own needs and opportunities. We are finding, more and more, that these evangelists are used widely in the diocese, as individuals and in teams, even though they are based in parishes and work under the direction of the local incumbent. While evangelists must, of course, have the gift of sharing the gospel easily and naturally wherever they find themselves, they cannot do it all themselves. This is why their task is also to help other people to share their faith, to make sure that evangelism is on the agenda of the parish and deanery and generally to enable the whole church to be mission-minded.

We are delighted, of course, that many other dioceses are

also making provision for this ministry. The Church of England, too, at the national level, has a scheme for recognising evangelists who have a national or international profile.[16]

Some other models

There are, of course, many other models: the church as *servant* became a very important way of speaking about the church in the 1960s and 1970s. Here an attempt is made to overcome the distance between church and world. The church is seen as part of the world, but a part that has been called to serve. The inspiration for this model comes from Jesus' understanding of his own ministry when he declared that the Son of Man had come not to be served but to serve (Mark 10:45 and parallels). St Paul also understands his own vocation in terms of *diakonia* ('service') – Acts 20:24; 2 Corinthians 4:1; and so on – as well as those of his closest colleagues, such as Timothy and Phoebe (Romans 16:1; 1 Thessalonians 3:2).

Whether Acts 6 may still be understood as the institution of the diaconate, the church has always recognised the need for a ministry that focuses its role as servant. This may be in meeting both physical and spiritual need in the church and it may also be a vehicle for meeting need in the world.[17] It is increasingly being recognised, however, that deacons have other tasks as well. In New Testament times one of the primary meanings of the term *diakonos* was that of 'messenger'. From the time of Ignatius onwards, deacons were closely associated with the bishop in the administration of the church's affairs. Liturgically, deacons focus their task as messengers in the reading of the gospel. As they lead in the intercessions or prepare the eucharistic gifts, they bring their tasks as carers and as stewards to God in the context of worship. Once again, their role is to remind the whole people of God (including bishops and presbyters) of their calling to be messengers, stewards and servants.[18]

In addition to those who are ordained as deacons, many churches have developed diaconal-type lay ministries. These are very different from one another but include working with the homeless, with single-parent families, in the rehabilitation of offenders and with people who have one kind of addiction or another.

The model of the church as servant has become significant for those who see the church's task as promoting compassion, peace and justice, both locally and globally. They see the church not as an alternative society but as salt and light within wider human communities. The church is called to serve the world in which it finds itself and not to establish structures that distinguish it too sharply from the communities in which it is embedded. An obvious danger with this way of thinking is that it tends to identify the church so much with society at large that its distinctiveness is lost. The church can be seen to endorse a secular agenda that has another ideological basis and to have lost its prophetic dimension. Such a situation was sometimes seen with churches in the communist world. They seemed servants not in the sense of loving and truthful ministry but as beholden to the regime, with little independence of thought and action. Doubtless, some of these constraints were unavoidable but, in other ways, church leadership was often compromised.

Biblical notions of service certainly do not imply capitulation to the present order. They include, rather, a fearless proclamation of God's will to the furthest corners of the earth (this is one of the tasks of the Servant in the Servant Songs of Isaiah – see, e.g., 49:6). Bringing justice to those who have been denied it and freedom from oppression are also tasks for the Servant (Isaiah 42:1; 61:1–4; cf. Luke 4:16–22). This is how Jesus understood his own ministry and, by extension, it is also the church's. In the New Testament Christians are called explicitly to be hospitable and peaceable, to provide for the basic necessities of even their enemies, to have a care for the poor, especially widows and orphans, to heal the sick and to seek the common good (Romans 12: 13, 18, 20; James 1:27; Acts 3:1–10, etc.; Galatians 6:10). Anyone who claims that the New Testament has only 'supernaturalist' and 'individualistic' notions of salvation has to reckon with the social teaching also found within its pages.

Another way of speaking about the church is to see it as *sacrament*. The church is not itself the kingdom of God, but it is a sacrament of that kingdom. It is a foretaste or pledge of God's reign of justice and love. On this view of the church, God is working out his purpose in a way that is sovereign and not beholden to any human institution. The community of those who are being redeemed is, however, an emblem of what is happening on a much grander scale throughout the cosmos. Through his grace, moreover, God allows us to work together with him in the fulfilment of his purposes (1 Corinthians 3:9; 2 Corinthians 6:1). Through faithfulness to God's word and the work of the Holy Spirit, the church conforms more and more to the kingdom, so that when it arrives in its fullness, the church can take its rightful place. Such a view is a useful corrective to those who see the church (or churches) as a merely human institution that is transitory and provisionally points to the kingdom but is never identified with it. In its present forms, we can agree that the church *is* provisional, but the church also has its place in the transformed order God is to bring about. Those wonderful images in the book of Revelation, where the redeemed are worshipping God in heaven (chs 7 and 8), and the image of the church as the bride of Christ (21:2, 9f; cf. Ephesians 5:25f) are certainly not pictures of a passing institution! In both Ephesians and Colossians the church is shown as part of God's eternal purposes (Ephesians 3:9–10; Colossians 1:18).

While the church as sacrament cannot be wholly identified with any institution, it is true that the church as sacrament is present wherever, according to Irenaeus, the Spirit of God is to be found.[19] The church of Jesus Christ will be present, then, to the extent that gospel truth and holiness are to be found, where people are being built up in Christ and where Christian love is expressed.

We have considered some of the different ways in which the church can be imagined. These are not exclusive but complementary. We have now to ask how biblical understandings of the essential features of being church, as well as these models, inform the different ways in which Christians are seeking to express their life together in our own times and in different cultures.

5. Ways of Being Church

CASE STUDY

In the middle of what used to be a quarry a new residential community is emerging. What should the churches do? Should the new residents go to existing local churches or should there be a new church in the quarry itself? The local authorities are quite sympathetic to a new church but they would want it to be ecumenical and, perhaps, even provide facilities for non-Christian faiths. What should the Church of England do, given that it will be the main funder? Should it provide an Anglican building, which other churches are welcome to use, or should it go for a fully ecumenical church, even if it takes longer? Should the building look *like a church or should it be a multipurpose building with architecture to match? How far should hospitality to people of other faiths extend? If it is all right for those of another faith to use ancillary buildings for social reasons, can they ever worship on church property and are there any occasions when Christians can pray with them?*[1] *As the church faces up to these questions about the use of buildings, we realise there are even more fundamental questions about how to be church today.*

In some parts of the world, the church finds itself in highly mobile situations. In others, it is isolated and under threat. In some parts there is an abundance of Christians engaged in ministry. In others, there is a paucity of ministers. All of these factors have led people to rethink 'ways of being church' that are related particularly to their culture or context. Some have emphasised the need for the church's life to be expressed in small and intimate Christian communities that are, nevertheless, open to a wide range of participation.[2] Others have tried to reorient the congregation for mission and service and there are yet others who see the church's agenda as drawn from the world and who see alliances with people of goodwill as a priority.

If they can't, we will

No one can deny that the earliest and most creative thinking about re-expressing the life of the church in recent times arose in Latin America (and possibly also the Philippines). The Base Ecclesial Community, as it came to be called, has its origins in the twin perceptions that if the institutional church (in this case, mostly the Roman Catholic Church) could not deliver an effective ministry to the urban poor in their *favelas* (shanty towns) and to the rural poor in their isolated settlements, then the people themselves must be mobilised for ministry and mission in their own context. The other perception was that such mobilisation is necessary if the church is to be an advocate of the poor and if it is to challenge structural injustice and exploitation on its own doorstep, as well as more widely.[3]

People got together to pray, to study the Bible, to celebrate their faith and to reflect on the situation around them. It did not much matter where they began: some began with the Bible and were driven out in mission to the people around them. Others began by being active in the community and were driven to the Bible as they sought the transformation of their own society. In the context of their life together, they discovered that God was speaking to them as they brought together the horizon of the Bible and the horizon of their community with its opportunities and problems.[4] They *wanted* to be a voice for the voiceless and to struggle for justice, peace and compassion. Out of this ferment arose liberation theology as an attempt to contextualise the good news in the lives of the very poor: What is good news for the poor in a specific social and political context? What resources do the Bible and Christian Tradition provide for the liberation of the poor from their oppressors? How do we move from an overindividualised idea of sin to a more corporate one? Is it possible to relate the Bible's teaching to the various spiritualities of the poor? How far can we go?

Different writers have, of course, given different answers to such questions, but there is a generic similarity as well. All reiterate the importance of reading the Bible in the light of particular circumstances. All emphasise God's special concern for the poor and those on the margins of society. All seek to equip Christian communities so that they can be advocates for social justice. It is true that some writers rely too heavily on Marxist social and economic analyses. This has led them to underrate the role of initiative and enterprise in changing the condition of the poor. They have been too much in thrall to grand deterministic theories that lay the entire blame for the condition of the poor on big business, state corruption and greedy landlords. There is no denying the reality of these forces but we need also, on the one hand, to recognise the ability of the poor to change their own situation and, on the other, elements in their own culture and background that prevent change.

A major criticism of liberation theology, as a whole, has been its neglect of the spirituality of the poor. The focus has been so much on economic and social change that the spiritual gifts and needs of the poor have been neglected. In countries like Brazil the result has been that the poor are turning massively to Pentecostal movements that offer the possibility of community life and support but also seek to nurture the spirit and cater specifically for the need to experience a transcendent dimension in life. Some, at least, of these movements are committed to a holistic view of mission, seeking change in their society, ministering to the daily needs of their people and encouraging a study of the Bible and reflection on the life of Jesus that is closely related to people's situation.[5]

Increasingly, leaders in the movement are admitting that activism in the social area and in political protest resulted in less emphasis on worship, study of the Bible and personal devotion. This must, of course, be true but we must not forget the great flowering of worship and celebration that accompanied the origins of the movement. Leonardo Boff tells us, for example, how in the absence of a priest, local congregations began to organise love feasts *they* called the Lord's Supper. These were basically a celebration of their life together and resulted in the breaking of the bread and drinking from the cup. The lay co-ordinator of each community tended to preside over those events. The communities were insistent that this was not the 'Mass'. For that a priest was necessary and when one was available, they were glad to co-operate with him. The Second Vatican Council had, however, declared that every local Christian community must be eucharistic, and yet the rule of celibacy in the Western church made this impossible. What were lay folk to do? They invented (or, rather, reinvented) the Lord's Supper with their community leader as the president.[6] The eucharistic overtones of this rite are unmistakable. That this is not an issue limited to Latin America is shown by writers like Thomas O'Loughlin who point to the similar needs of churches in the Western world also facing a shortage of clergy. Churches that do not insist on celibacy for ordained ministry can, of course, identify leaders in local communities and prepare them for duly authorised ordained ministry. We shall see later that this may, in fact, be the right way of viewing ordained ministry in local communities and of retaining the centrality of the Eucharist for these communities.[7]

Small Christian communities

Latin America's base communities have inspired a number of experiments all over the world. As Christians recover the importance of community in the life of the church, they turn increasingly to focusing their own discipleship in small communities with an intensive life. Peter Price tells us that such communities should be drawn from a range of ages, professions and social backgrounds. They should be open and accessible, particularly to those who may not be welcome elsewhere. They should be long term as an expression of a common life, and there should be provision for celebrating this life together. To these we may add the necessity not only of *hospitality* as an aspect of mission but of *embassy*, of going out as a community, or on behalf of the community, to witness to the gospel and its values. It is necessary, of course, for such communities to network with one another and also with the wider church. Such communities should not be confused with small groups that come together for specific activity, such as Bible study, which may be temporary, like-minded and not mission-oriented. Small Christian communities will, typically, integrate people of different kinds and operate over a range of activities. They will provide a focus for belonging that will not be exclusive (e.g. in relation to the congregation) but will, nevertheless, be strong.[8]

Cell churches

One expression of Small Christian Communities (SCCs), which has found widespread acceptance among evangelicals, is the cell church. It was pioneered in South-East Asia where it has increased the already rapid growth of the church. In his recent book[9] Canon Michael Green gives a breathtaking account of this movement. I know personally one of the congregations he describes: St Patrick's, Tawau, in Sabah, East Malaysia. I knew it as a rather charismatic and predominantly Chinese Anglican church in the timberland of Malaysia. Even then it was growing. Now, claims Michael Green, its growth is exponential and the reason is cells. Sunday attendance was 600 in 1990 but by 2000 it had grown to over 3,000! Archdeacon Albert Vun, the parish priest, believes it is because of the 315 cells the church has established. Every cell, seen as a church in its immediate neighbourhood, has lightly trained leadership that is flexible in changing situations, and when the cell exceeds fifteen members, it multiplies into two. Unlike other SCCs, cells may be heterogeneous, with a mix of people belonging to them, or homogeneous, with cells for young people being a runaway favourite.

According to Michael Green cell churches are effective because they create caring communities of a size most people find easy to understand. They are effective in church growth because people can be easily invited to a warm and friendly group. People in the cell are encouraged to exercise the gifts God has given them. A close fellowship is effective for the nurture of new Christians and for developing any gifts of leadership that may be discerned. Although cells are usually related to an existing congregation, they can also be a way of planting churches in new or previously unchurched areas.

Green emphasises the need in the cell to create warm interpersonal relationships but also to make worship and teaching central. Members are encouraged to go out to meet human need and to witness to their faith. When newcomers are brought, there is a special programme so that they may feel at home.

Green is too much of an old campaigner not to know that there are weaknesses as well: there is a tendency to split off from the parent body for minor doctrinal reasons, teaching is at a minimal level, and sometimes control from the 'top' can asphyxiate the cell. For these reasons cells should never be seen as adequate manifestations of the church in themselves. Like other SCCs, they too need to belong to a wider network where deeper teaching and worship can be provided and the assumptions, perhaps, of members challenged.

Small Christian communities today correspond to the church in the home of the New Testament period. We have seen that this *family* aspect of the church is an essential manifestation of the church but is not sufficient in itself. It needs the church in the city, or the wider community, if it is to flourish, and also, of course, it needs the fellowship, the prayers and the teaching of the church throughout the world and in every age.

Missionary congregations

New thinking about small Christian communities has been paralleled by reflection on the church set in a larger area and gathering together a number of people corresponding to the church in a city or town of the New Testament period. Bishop Peter Price, himself a great advocate of small communities, has this to say about the parish:

> from the word *paroikia* comes our word *parish*, meaning 'the strangers who dwell alongside'. The *parish church* then is the 'gathering of called out ones who, in the name of Jesus Christ, seek the welfare of the strangers who dwell alongside'. To this I want to say 'wowee!' – even if the definition is a bit quaint when put in this quite literal way! Because such an understanding reveals to us *what* the church is, *why* it is, and *who* it is for.[10]

Not surprisingly, it is Bishop Lesslie Newbigin, a great missionary, who has reflected most cogently on the congregation as the interpreter of the gospel to the community around. As the Christian congregation rehearses the word and the works of Jesus, exhibits his risen life in the sacraments, renews itself again and again in these ways, it draws others into this life. In doing so, it provides them also with the 'lenses' needed to interpret an ambiguous world.

A congregation will be an effective 'hermeneutic' of the gospel if it is a community of praise and thanksgiving. As another bishop, Stephen Sykes, has said, those who praise God in the congregation are led to praise him in the world.[11] It will be a community of truth, living by that true story which reveals the purpose of this world and tells us something of our destiny. In doing this, it will have to battle with other accounts of our existence that deny purpose or belittle human dignity. It will be deeply involved in all that promotes the common good in the neighbourhood. Its members will be trained, supported and nourished in their task of being a royal priesthood. That is to say, they will be enabled to bring God to the world and the world to God. It is the task of the ministerial priesthood to make sure that this enabling is happening. They exercise their specific ministry so that all of the baptised can exercise theirs. Such a community will be an example of mutual support and responsibility, setting its face against individualism even when it is about spiritual fulfilment. Above all, it will be a community of hope. Hope in making things better in this life (as the Christian Aid slogan has it 'We believe in life before death') but also hope in the fulfilment of our deepest spiritual longings for fellowship with God, the source of all that exists. These communities of praise, truth and hope will make a difference to the world and, in doing so, will most effectively communicate the good news of Jesus Christ.[12]

As always, Newbigin has drawn our attention to a much neglected aspect of the congregation: its missionary nature. If Newbigin has made the headlines, it is Canon Robert Warren who has developed a systematic strategy for *building missionary congregations* or, to put it differently, *growing healthy churches.* Such churches will be places where people encounter the living God and this will, once and for all, affect their style of life and the choices they make. Their agenda will come from waiting on God but will have an outward focus. An enabling leadership will result in a participative laity. They will be a loving community that sees discipleship as long term. They will not necessarily, therefore, go for the excitement of the moment but will aim to do the ordinary things well.

If a church really is going to be missionary, it needs to establish its priorities immediately both internally and in relation to the wider community. For Robert Warren this means that decision-makers, like the Parochial Church Council (PCC), will have to give up their 'churchy' focus on priest plus stipend plus building, and reorientate themselves to something like faith plus community plus action. Naturally, exactly how this happens will vary from place to place but there are common elements. There has to be a commitment to *effective* Christian presence, not *mere* presence, which can be irrelevant or, worse, actually alienating. Being there should make a difference to those around. Such presence should be grounded in a deepened and deepening spirituality. Missionaries are of no use whatever until they have such a deep and infectious spirituality. Now the ground is ready for proclamation. This does not mean, of course, getting on to a soapbox and talking *at* people. Very often it will mean making sure that there is added gospel value in all that the church does for the community. It will mean making sure there are bridges between the church's presence and community service, on the one hand, and its spirituality and witness on the other. So often we find that churches are very active in the use made of their buildings and in the involvement of their members in the community, but we do not ask the question 'What connection is there between these and the worshipping, witnessing life of the church?' Sometimes the answers can be quite simple.

Do church hall noticeboards, for example, post times of services in church along with a warm invitation to come? Many of those who use these halls do not make any connection in their minds between them and the living church next door. Is there any Christian literature or portions of Scripture available in such buildings? We can never tell when someone who is lonely, going through a crisis or in some other kind of difficulty will need this kind of help. When churches have holiday clubs or take the elderly or housebound for a much-needed outing, is there any Christian content to such events? Is even grace said before meals or, perhaps, a little epilogue at the end of the day? As is so often said today, it is important to make people feel they *belong* but, then, also to nurture *belief* so that they have all the resources for living.

CASE STUDY

St Levi's is in a fairly rundown residential area, within which are schools, a women's prison and a large 'sink' estate. When the new parish priest arrived, she first of all got the congregation to do an 'audit' of their worship: was it welcoming, accessible, edifying? The result was simple but dignified liturgical services with a touch of 'renewal' music. She then invited a team to help her with prison work. The result is a vibrant and growing Christian fellowship. Gradually, she has been able to train a team for visiting, baptism and marriage preparation and to lead in worship. A women's group has now started an Alpha course with over a dozen attending. From a seemingly hopeless situation, we can see signs of life emerging in a church that is focused in its spiritual and worshipping life but also outward-looking in mission.[13]

Raymond Fung comes from a background in industrial mission in his native Hong Kong. For a while, he was at the World Council of Churches' evangelism desk (wonderful to know they have one!) and he is now back in Hong Kong. The Isaiah vision has come from both his local and his worldwide experience. He realises that the world wants to know what Christians are about and whether it has anything to do with them. Fung produces a 'minimalist' agenda from that great vision of human welfare found in Isaiah 65:20–23:

- Children do not die.
- Old people live in dignity.
- Those who build houses live in them.
- Those who plant, eat the fruit.

He has found that such an agenda can be a basis for partnership with many people of goodwill in a whole host of different situations. That Christians *have* such an agenda is in itself attractive to many and this can lead them to explore further into the faith (careful provision must be made for this). When the partnership around the agenda is to be celebrated, worship may be a natural part of such a celebration. There is no doubt that the agenda works – up to a point. Through it, it is possible to involve a large number of people in service and even in community celebration. The faith is shared and some people are drawn into the community of faith. It can be, however, a painfully slow process and, in some places, it works at one level but not at others.

The Institute for Basic Adult Development and Training (IBADAT – the acronym means 'worship' in Arabic, Persian and Urdu) is a voluntary organisation working in the urban and rural areas of Pakistan's Punjab. Its work of awareness-raising, literacy, training and public health among the poorest of the poor has attracted strong support from Muslims as well as Christians. The partnership is centred on continuing dialogue where Christians listen to their Muslim friends as well as share their faith with them. They are able, from time to time, to celebrate their work and to praise God for it.

The Isaiah vision can be the basis for co-operation at any level but, perhaps, the most important is that of the local church and the community around it. It is here, most of all, that a difference can be made. This is how Fung believes a positive invitation to get involved should be made to a wide cross-section of the community:

> The God we believe in is the one who protects the children, empowers the elderly and walks with working men and women. As Christians, we wish to act accordingly. We believe you share in similar concerns. Let us join hands.[14]

An inside-out church

CASE STUDY

Andrew Mawson is a United Reformed Church minister who, when he arrived in Whitechapel, East London, was told that he had come to close the church (how often we have heard this story!). In the first few months of his ministry, he simply went around the area visiting people and asking them, 'What do you want the church to do for you?' Naturally, he got a long list of answers and from that he set about prioritising and making the church more responsive to those around it.

The church building is now used every day of the week. There are training courses for jobs available in that part of London. The church has become a place for meeting in an area where there are few such places for people to meet about a common concern. Andrew and the church leadership have been able to take some of the problems of the community to the local authority and even to central government. Mechanisms have been developed and events take place to ensure that the poorest are heard by those who make decisions. The church has become a focus for what Andrew calls 'Christian entrepreneurial activity'. Not everyone may like the term but Andrew is certainly a social entrepreneur and is glad to call himself that.

The 'inside-out church' exists not simply to continue its worship nor even to deepen the faith of its members but for the sake of the world outside. To a very great extent its agenda has been set by the wider community. In fact, this has also led to a more vigorous church community. There is, however, a risk involved in this kind of approach. The minister may end up as an advocate for every social cause with no time to nurture the congregation, which may, indeed, all but disappear. If this approach is to succeed, it must be built on preparation of the congregation, on prayer, perhaps on partnership with other churches for the spiritual and material resources that may be needed and on an effective system of support and oversight for the minister.

Houses of hope and of sharing

Korea is a rapidly urbanising country: more than 30 per cent of the population live in the capital, Seoul, alone. Not surprisingly, the authorities have not managed to keep up with this rapid immigration into the cities and there are huge residential areas, which, though not quite slums (this is Korea, after all!), are bereft of facilities like education, social services, adequate medical assistance and even, in some cases, basic sanitation (how many diseases does that alone cause?).

The churches in Korea, and particularly the Anglican Church, began a ministry in these areas that was, at first, essentially about delivering basic services to the people, many of whom had recently arrived in the city. They were offered advice about employment rights, some adult education, a place to meet to air community concerns, and so on. An old-fashioned way, perhaps, of engaging with the poor but, you see, the poor hit back! They began to ask, 'Why are you doing all these things for us?' The churches, however reluctantly, had to respond, 'Because we are Christians!' 'Well,' said the people, 'why don't you worship with us then?' In this way these 'houses of hope' became centres of worship and evangelism as well. Increasingly, the residents are taking control of these houses, relying less and less on the outside world for the building of a genuinely Christian community in their area. In addition to being houses of hope, they are now houses of sharing as well!

Curiously enough, I am reminded here of Ann Morisy's insight that Christians should do nothing that merely duplicates what the social, educational or medical services can do.[15] There must be added value whether in content, witness to Christ or attitude. The churches in Korea were offering welfare services without this distinctively Christian added value. It is to the credit of the people that they saw through this as only half a commitment. They wanted the *whole* gospel, which met all their need.

Well, we might say, the 'houses of hope and sharing' were an accidental, an unplanned church planting! Most church plants are not like that at all. They are most carefully planned (or should be) and there is usually an extensive period of consultation, prayer and motivation before a plant can begin life. I suppose that, in the Anglican context, the most usual sort of church plant is still one *within* the geographical unit of the parish. An area is identified that is distant or inaccessible in relation to the parish church or, perhaps, it has a distinctive culture of its own. Often a suitable building, such as a school or community centre, is used. If the plant is to succeed, there must be a determined effort by the planting congregation to transfer enough human and financial resources over a sufficient period of time. Many plants fail because those who have gone to be members lose their nerve and return to the safety of their previous congregation.

Sometimes incumbents and PCCs have not counted the cost before venturing into these risky waters. It is important, nevertheless, that such plants should be encouraged if significant parts of the community are not effectively to be unchurched. 'A church for every community in the land' is an empty boast if it boils down to there being a church in a given geographical area, without any reference to accessibility or culture. Roads and railway lines, social or private housing, accents and occupations all constitute significant barriers that should make us at least think whether a church plant is appropriate.

Church planting across parish boundaries, and sometimes even across diocesan boundaries, is taking place with greater frequency. Sometimes a parish may ask another to help in the revival of the congregation through the transfer of people and skills or to help it begin something new. At other times another parish, or even a group of like-minded people, may have a burden for reaching a certain kind of population living in the parish where the planting is to take place. The consent of the incumbent and, in the case of plants across dioceses, the bishop, will be necessary and will have to be negotiated. Sometimes bishops are only too glad to be party to a plan that will bring new Christian life and witness to an area. Where it is necessary to reach a particular section of the community, a plant may be declared an extra-parochial place of worship with the support of the local incumbent and PCC, though it should be noticed that, under the Extra-Parochial Ministry Measure 1967, the bishop may license a priest to officiate in any institution, public or charitable, with or without the support of the parish in which such an institution is located.

CASE STUDY

St Alban's used to be a chapel on an army base. The army has now withdrawn and the accommodation is being used by the local council to house 'problem families'. The parish in which the chapel is geographically located felt unable to provide the necessary resources for a plant. A neighbouring parish then stepped in and offered to 'kick-start' the project. With the approval of the bishop, they provided a basic team to visit, to lead in worship and, eventually, to bring some basic facilities to a deeply deprived area. With diocesan support, the geographical parish has now resumed its responsibilities for the area and there is a full-time lay worker (still funded by the diocese) at the plant. If additional housing is built, the plant may yet become a conventional district and, possibly, a parish.

Breaking New Ground, the Church of England's report on church planting, emphasises the need for long-term diocesan and deanery planning and consultation if plants are not to be the enthusiasm of the moment, here today and gone tomorrow.[16] There is also the need for long-term commitment, so that when the romance wears off, people will stick with a plain building, few people, little music, and so on, and not pine for the fleshpots they have left behind. For those who go, there is a need to understand the needs of the locality and to befriend the local people. As Bishop Azariah of India said to the missionaries of his time, 'You have given your goods to feed the poor. You have given your bodies to be burned. We ask also for *love*. Give us Friends!'[17] Love and friendship is primary but there may have to be body-burning too! As elsewhere, there is no room here for 'hit and run' missionaries. We often criticise Victorian missionaries for their narrow outlook, their racism and their triumphalism. Such criticism may indeed be right but we must not forget that they often gave their lives in the service of Christ. Theirs was an incarnational ministry at a cost almost unimaginable to us. It was a ministry of learning, of advocacy on behalf of the poor, and of sacrifice. Today we think we can do in a few months what people, more committed than we are, could not do in a lifetime.

Once a plant has taken place there is a need for periodic evaluation. In addition to the parish, parish development officers, archdeacons and bishops may also have to become involved. Is there continuing commitment? Are there sufficient resources? Is there appropriate engagement with the local community? If it is clear that a plant is not succeeding, it is better to end the experiment with a clean break rather than continue with a 'lame duck' that affects the general credibility of the church.

Growing churches

Church plants generally involve the transfer of people and resources from one place to another – in the case of transplants, entire congregations can be moved from one location to another. There is, however, another approach to try in some situations. It is subtly different from church planting and may be termed something like 'growing a church' in a locality. Typically, it will involve trying to find a family or two who have some church connections, even if it is outside the immediate area. The next step might be to help them meet from time to time (every month?) for Bible study, prayer and waiting on God. From this, very slowly, a church can emerge.

We have a large and 'upmarket' housing estate built by some American developers. The national press said that it was just like an English village *except* that there was no church! When the developers were asked about it they said that their survey among residents had not revealed any desire for a place of worship (I wonder what the questions were?). For a while we accepted this, even if we were saddened by it. Then somebody had the bright idea that the church should carry out its own survey. This revealed some starkly different results: 60 per cent or so of the households said they were Church of England, about 15 per cent declared themselves Roman Catholic and a further 15 per cent Free Church of one kind or another. Many *had* wondered about access to a church, if only for the occasional offices, and some were concerned about the spiritual education of their children.

At about this time a very few Christian families (attached to a variety of churches outside the area) had started to meet, preparing themselves for a coming mission. A sympathetic Head arrived for the local county school who was more than happy that the school should be used for the larger gatherings at festival times and other major occasions. Christmas, Easter and Harvest services have been particularly well attended. In addition to the bigger gatherings, two small groups meet weekly, one on a weekday morning and the other on a weekday evening. A priest-evangelist has recently been assigned to work with the lay people and our hope is that in five years' time there will be a viable Christian presence on the development. We have no building yet and one of the unanswered questions is whether we need a parsonage on the site or a church building – given the high costs of the place both are not an option in the short term.

In the Thames Gateway area we are faced with some massive demographic shifts. New business is moving into the area and new housing developments will bring a substantial number of new people into the area. The local churches are preparing to reach out to some of these, but in entirely new residential developments we will have to consider whether to plant churches (with considerable input from elsewhere) or to grow churches with the help of skilled evangelists and pastors. Perhaps it will be a mixture of both, as well as drawing on some of the other ways of being church that we have considered.

The Homogeneous Unit Principle

Since the days of Matthew Ricci and Robert Nobili in the sixteenth and seventeenth centuries, missionaries have made attempts to reach resistant groups of people in ways that caused the least disruption to their culture. Ricci was notably successful in his attempts to reach the Chinese, and Nobili also achieved limited success in evangelising and discipling people from the higher castes in Hinduism.[18] Since then, missionaries like Donald MacGavran have developed methods not only of reaching people in this way but even of forming churches in their midst that do not require them to cross boundaries of caste or ethnicity. MacGavran's statement that people 'like to become Christians without crossing racial, linguistic or class barriers' has given rise to the so-called *Homogeneous Unit Principle* (HUP). In missionary terms the 'peoples group' concept embodies this principle. Mission is now not directed so much at individuals or even at a geographical area with a differentiated population. It is focused on a particular group, large or small, that sees itself as consisting of people with a similar background and interests.[19]

The church-planting report, to which I have referred, tells us about DAWN (Discipling A Whole Nation), which aims to plant a church in 'every cultural group' within the nation. In the same way, the Tomorrow Project speaks of 'highly customised' churches catering for existing or new networks.[20] The Tomorrow Project report highlights the confusion there can be between using the HUP for reaching out to people and turning it into a cornerstone of ecclesiology. We are already used to student missions, nurses' Christian associations, fellowships for lawyers and even for those in prison! It is easier to interpret the gospel to like-minded people and, to some extent, it is beneficial to nurture them in their new-found faith in such groups, but what is an effective principle in *mission* is not necessarily the best way of being *church*. By all means reach out to professional groups, parents of school children, teenagers and people in the city. To some extent, it will be possible to nurture them in such groups but, in the end, those who reach out and the reached will have to come to terms with the universality of the church and this demands *heterogeneity* not homogeneity.

We have to get used to rubbing shoulders with people *un*like us: black, brown, yellow or white, young and old, rich or poor, men or women. If the church is fundamentally about breaking down the barriers human sin has erected, we cannot be content with homogeneous churches, unless they are an accident of geography (Galatians 3:28; Ephesians 2:11–22; Colossians 3:11). Even where language, liturgical tradition and music divide, ways must be found for people to come together regularly, as well as to be distinctive. It is absolutely right for churches to make provision for people from different backgrounds and even with different tastes, but this cannot be at the expense of the church's unity. There must be times and places for togetherness and times and places for distinctiveness.

CASE STUDY

In an industrial city in the Midlands, Punjabi Christians gather on a Sunday afternoon to worship in their own language, using their rich folk-music tradition for their time of praise. People from other cultural and racial groups are welcome to join them. This is not, however, a homogeneous church, for those Punjabi Christians also belong to the local Anglican parish and play their full part in it. Through coming together regularly and having times when they can celebrate their distinctiveness (but always in an inclusive way), each group is able to enrich the other and the church as a whole. Let us then have fellowships of people from an ethnic or professional background, of young people and of men or women, but let us call them church only when they are all put together and when they come together. As distinctive groups they may be important aspects of the church's work of outreach and nurture but they are not, in themselves, church. That requires diversity, learning from one another and tolerating one another.

In the nature of the case, we have been looking at *new* ways of being church. Our interest has been very much in how people are responding to fresh and challenging situations in terms of their life together as Christians. This is, of course, entirely legitimate, but it should not give the impression that these are the *only* attractive ways of being church today. Robert Warren has drawn our attention to the growing tension between inherited 'modes' of being church and emerging ones.[21] We should recognise, however, that some people are entirely comfortable in the inherited ways and, indeed, there are still some who are drawn to the church through these ways. The enormous popularity of Christmas crib and carol services, of harvest and of songs of praise suggests that people have a soft spot for what they see as 'traditional'. Churches are absolutely right to use these means to reach such people. Many are drawn to cathedral-type services with formality and 'BBC Radio 3' music, and yet others to a sense of history and of rootedness provided by the great liturgical occasions such as the Easter Vigil and all that follows it. As far as I can see, there will always be people who are drawn to these inherited ways. There may be fewer of them but they will still be there. This is why the churches need to respond with maximum flexibility – trying to meet the needs of different groups in a locality – but without sacrificing integrity and the essential unity of God's people in a given place.

CASE STUDY

A church in the 'stockbroker belt' has a traditional Anglican sung Eucharist with robed choirs and vestments at 9.30 a.m. on Sundays. This attracts two hundred or so mainly middle-aged people but the (younger) parents of the choristers are there also.

Those who want the rest of the day free come to this service, regardless of their private preferences. Then at 11.00 a.m. there is a noisy family service with the barest 'Service of the Word' structure (sometimes followed by a shortened service of Holy Communion). Naturally, there are lots of families present with maximum participation, 'renewal' music and considerable use of audio-visual material in the teaching programme. What is ostensibly directed at children is often most appreciated by adults! This is followed sometimes by a 'bring and share' lunch to which all are invited, though only some stay. These tend to be the single people, the DINKS ('double income, no kids') and some older couples. After a prayer meeting at about 5 p.m., there is a youth 'event' in church led entirely by the young people. This is not all loud music and leather jackets. Some of it is very reflective and raises sharp questions about Christian discipleship in an unjust and oppressive world. Many present are about to make decisions that will affect the rest of their lives. Here, then, is a church trying to respond to the variety found in a community that may appear monochrome from the outside but isn't like that at all.

6. What Kind of Ministry Does the Church Require?

Although the number of ordinands is going up, the number of stipendiary clergy is still going down. This is because more and more are retiring at sixty-five or thereabouts rather than staying on until they are seventy. Dioceses have to deploy the decreasing number available to them in the most strategic way possible.

CASE STUDY

Recently we have had to bring two parishes together. They now share a stipendiary priest. In terms of church tradition, the parishes are quite different, although the socio-economic profile is similar. Both have good potential for developing local leadership. The parish priest, assisted by diocesan training staff, is busy trying to develop ministry teams in each. These are essential if he is not to be driven from pillar to post trying to cope with all the demands of ministry in both parishes.

One of the parishes is further on than the other: they are more used to leadership being exercised by lay people and there are one or two lay people who would make suitable ordained ministers for work in the parish. How is their vocation to be discerned? Should they put themselves forward or should the parish, or, indeed, the wider church, call them out? How will other lay leaders feel when this happens, and how can they be affirmed in their ministry? Will there be any difference in the ministry of the locally ordained ministers and the priest in charge, or will they just supplement what he does?

Will the other parish 'catch up' with the first, or will it develop another pattern of ministry altogether? How can it be encouraged to discern the gifts that can be exercised for the building up of the congregation and for its mission?

As the parish priest, the diocesan staff and the parishes struggle with these questions, are there any principles to guide them? How are they to apply these to the contexts in which they are working?

We have seen how the shape of the church is affected by movements of thought and of life in the world. As it responds, or perhaps reacts, to these movements, its shape is altered for good or ill – it may become expansive, pluriform and creative, or it may be that it shrinks back and within, monocultural and custom-dominated ('we have always done it this way'). We have seen also how the shape of the church is determined from the 'inside' – by what has been handed down from the beginning, how the church has received this and how it seeks to understand it today. We saw that what has been handed down requires us to believe that there are certain essential ways of being church that are good for every age and every culture, but, alongside this truth, we saw also that the church is a mystery and that no particular way of looking at it exhausts the reality. This led us not only to explore various models, metaphors and images of the church but also new ways of being church.

The global and the local

We find ourselves, on the one hand, in a highly global situation. People have access to instantaneous information. They are increasingly aware of the options of belief and of lifestyle available to them. At the same time, there is increasing fragmentation. No one view is regarded as privileged and, even in fairly local situations, people live cheek by jowl with many different worldviews and value systems. They find 'community' not so much in terms of where they live but in 'networks' related to their work, leisure or commitments (such as green issues, human rights or world development – to take some of the more worthwhile ones). Alongside this new diversity, there are, of course, the traditional divides of race, ethnicity, language and social class. Depending on where they are located churches are, more or less, affected by these divides as well.

In such a world the church cannot just go on doing what it has always done. In the early church the evangelists and the apologists developed a number of approaches depending on the kind of people they were addressing. They spoke to Jewish people in one way, to the educated Greeks in another and to those outside the Graeco-Roman milieu in yet another.[1] Today also, the church is present in a number of cultural situations and needs to respond appropriately. The lesson from the church's missionary history is that the gospel *affirms* something of people's beliefs, points to the *ful-*

filment of their authentic spiritual aspirations in Christ and *challenges* all that is not according to God's will.

The churches can still have significant *rapport* with people, particularly at times of transition: people may laugh at the 'hatch, match and dispatch' aspect of the church's role in society but these remain significant moments of outreach. These, and other opportunities, should not be wasted by assuming that people will inevitably share the culture dominant in the church. Each opportunity should, rather, be seen as an occasion for outreach that resonates with the culture of the people being reached. Preparation for marriage and the marriage service, for instance, should recognise where people are culturally and, at the same time, bring distinctive Christian teaching to bear on the preparation and the service itself.

What is true of the occasional offices is true also of regular patterns of worship in the church. If people of different cultures, ages and interests are to become actively involved in worship, it is obvious that provision will have to be made for a variety of styles of worship and for variety within particular services. The need for 'common prayer' and 'common memory' will have to be balanced with the need for such greater flexibility.

Many church-related organisations are active in outreach to and discipling among people in various professional and leisure networks. The institutional churches need not only to 'own' such work but to seek to draw on it for their own congregational life and its renewal. Such a ministry also moves us away from the 'Sunday morning only' scenario to seeing how people can be helped to grow at their place of work. Alpha and Emmaus are showing us the importance of hospitality for Christian witness and learning. Being active with a Christian organisation in housing or in training helps church members to relate to the wider community. These organisations also often help us to see how church buildings can be made available and adaptable so that they can be used for a variety of activities.

How has ministry been shaped?

What kind of *ministry* will such an outward-looking, missionary-minded church need? It will need the ministry of *all the baptised*. Clergy alone, or even ministerial teams, cannot make a church missionary. The whole congregation has to be mobilised. For this to happen, gifts will have to be *discerned*, people will have to *learn* how to use their gifts for the building up of the church and for mission. People will have to be *confident* in sharing their faith and the church will need to learn how to be *prophetic* in the struggle for peace, justice and compassion in each community and the world over.

In the Christian way we are bound to seek help for today's problems by looking at what the foundational events and documents have to tell us and then relating that to our own situation. What patterns of ministry are there in the New Testament and the early church? Are they of value to us today? It has to be said straight away that neither the forms of ministry nor language about them are set in stone in the early period. There is, in fact, considerable flexibility to be found in a highly dynamic and growing situation. Even so, principles can be discerned and patterns recognised that may be of relevance today.[2]

The New Testament has, as its point of departure, a theology of gracious gift.[3] That is to say, God gives to the church whatever is needed to sustain the church's own life and to equip it for mission. Passages that list the gifts God has given us emphasise that this is for the sake of the church's unity and mission. In 1 Corinthians 12 this is particularly related to the unity of the Trinity – the one God, from whom these gifts flow, builds up in this way the unity of God's people. Both this passage and Romans 12 also use the 'body' image – the different gifts are for the sake of building up the one body of Christ. In these passages, and also in Ephesians 4, the gifts God has given are related to tasks or ministries in the church. Indeed, from 1 Corinthians 12:28 we seem to be moving towards offices that are, nevertheless, closely related to the gifts. Without the gift, it would not be possible to discharge the office.[4]

Two matters should be noticed here. The first is the sheer *variety* of ministries listed and, secondly, that we have not yet moved towards the specialisation we shall see later. The recovery of the insight that each of the baptised is a steward of whatever gift God has given (1 Peter 4:10) and that particular gifts have been given for leadership in the church must be seen in the light of these passages. Everyone has a gift and some have gifts especially necessary for the unity and the building up of the church. Authorised lay ministries, for example, need to be seen as the church's discernment of gifts and the enabling of those who have them to use them for the good of the whole church.

Again, it is against this background that we must examine the emergence of presbyter-bishops and deacons in the local churches. Elders or presbyters played a notable part in the

Judaism of Jesus' day. They were people of influence who had a say in how a local synagogue was run, and some, at least, had a role in the central councils of the Jews, such as the Sanhedrin. When the apostles came to appoint presbyters, and it is worth noting that it was the apostles and *not* the congregations who appointed them, they were both similar to and different from the Jewish elders.[5] They were similar in that they too were senior people of influence. They were different in that they seem to have had direct responsibility for teaching, pastoral care and worship. In Paul's speech to the Ephesian presbyters, Luke emphasises the pastoral role of these elders (Acts 20:18–35). This is also one of the passages that identifies elders (or presbyters) with bishops: Paul reminds the Ephesian elders that the Holy Spirit has made them shepherds (or bishops) to feed the church of God purchased with Christ's own blood (1 Peter 5:2 may be another such passage, although the manuscripts differ about the exact words). This identification seems to continue in the Pauline letters where the bishops (plural) and deacons are mentioned as officers in the church at Philippi. The very early *Didache* (the Teaching of the Twelve Apostles) also mentions bishops and deacons as officers of the local church. The Pastoral Letters seem to give presbyters a much clearer role in teaching and leading the church and in the ordination of fellow-elders (1 Timothy 5:17–18; 4:14). The office of bishop is now in the singular and is, perhaps, being distinguished from that of the presbyter (although Titus 1:5–9 seems to go back to the original understanding).

We saw earlier how the office of deacon focuses the calling of the whole church to be servants of God, proclaimers of the gospel and helpers of those in any kind of need. From the beginning, deacons assist the president at worship and go out with the eucharistic elements to the ill and the housebound. They are stewards of the church's resources. Even though they came to have a wider (and very influential) role in the church, they were, in the early period, primarily officials of the local Christian community.

It is within a gifted church, with a variety of ministries, that vocations to ordained ministry, of presbyters and deacons, should first be discerned. The New Testament and the early writings are clear that these are local ministers. They arise from and work in the local community, even if they are affirmed and commissioned by the wider church. Their training today should, therefore, take seriously the wider context of the church that commissions them *and* the local context that is to be the primary locus of their ministry.

If a truly distinctive diaconate is to re-emerge in our church, it will be because local churches see the need to give liturgical expression to their evangelism and service in the community. Deacons will have the specific task of relating the 'stewardship' (the *oikonomia*) of the church to its worship and the proclamation of the gospel. Those who are engaged in social service, in grass-roots evangelism or in ministries of listening, counselling and care, such as pastoral assistants or auxiliaries, may well be the ones who are called to be deacons in the church.

There will be others who are called to teach the faith, to bring the sacraments, as channels of grace, to the people, to lead and to preside over the community in love. Naturally, such vocations cannot be for the individual alone: the local and wider church will have their due part in discerning whether a person is truly called to be a deacon or presbyter in the church. Indeed, the initiative for such discernment may come from the local or wider church! Their preparation, too, must keep both horizons firmly in view: the local context must be taken very seriously. Indeed, it may provide a framework for the preparation. Questions raised from it will then be addressed with the assistance of theological disciplines such as biblical studies, church history or systematic theology. At the same time – because it is one of the responsibilities of the ordained to relate the local to the universal – the worldwide, the regional and the national dimensions will also have to be kept in mind.

In addition to these local ministries, however, there are other kinds of ministries to which we must now turn our attention. There are, for example, the ministries of apostles and 'apostolic delegates', of the prophets and teachers. Gordon Kuhrt rightly reminds us that the term 'apostle' means someone who is sent with authority and that Jesus himself is called 'apostle' (Hebrews 3:1).[6] Typically, though, it is the Twelve who are meant (Matthew 10:2; Acts 1; 1 Corinthians 15:5, 7; etc.). In addition, Paul calls himself an apostle, though with a great sense of unworthiness (1 Corinthians 15:9; 2 Corinthians 12:12; Galatians 1:1). Barnabas is called an apostle, along with Paul (Acts 14:14) and the couple (?) Andronicus and Junia are given the title in Romans 16:7. The *Didache* still knows of the itinerant 'apostles' and how they should be treated, though it may be that the meaning here is coming to be 'missionary' or 'evangelist' (11:3–6).

The 'apostolic delegates' are people like Timothy and Titus who have been given a special commission by an apostle such as Paul (1 Timothy 1:3; Titus 1:5). It is clear that they have general oversight of the church, including the appointment, remuneration and discipline of presbyters, deacons and other officers in the church. They are to supervise the church's worship and the teaching given in it, imitating the apostle himself in their personal lives.

Bishop Charles Gore, in his monumental work on the origins of Christian ministry, points out that the prophets are regularly ranked immediately after the apostles in the New Testament (1 Corinthians 12:28; Ephesians 4:11; etc.). In the *Didache* theirs appears to be an itinerant ministry of teaching, encouraging, warning and enabling. According to Gore, wherever they appear they become the chief ministers at worship. Already, though, the ministry is changing from an itinerant to a settled one.[7]

The ministries of apostles, apostolic delegates and of prophets and teachers were ministries of *oversight*, peripatetic or settled, that sought to keep the church united in truth, encouraged Christians to live according to the gospel and enabled them to fulfil their mission in their locality. When necessary, however, they also warned of danger and exercised discipline when needed.

It appears that in some churches, for example in Western Asia, there were bishops from the beginning who were regarded as the legitimate, if limited, successors of the apostles. The testimony of Ignatius and of Polycarp is extremely important in this respect. Ignatius (d. 108) wrote his letters as a condemned prisoner on his way from Antioch to Rome, where he was thrown to the lions. He certainly regarded the episcopate (along with the presbyterate and diaconate) as essential to the church, and he also regarded it as already universal.[8] Such a 'developed' view of the church's ministry is quite remarkable as it must reflect practice in Antioch from towards the end of the first century!

There were other churches, however, that appear to have had a more presbyteral organisation. It is interesting that even Ignatius, when writing to the church in Rome, does not mention bishops, and Clement of Rome writing to the Corinthians assumes a presbyteral form of government in that church. At the same time, churches that took an 'essentialist' view of episcopacy, such as the Asian ones, seem to have enjoyed fraternal relations with the European ones, which did not. Ignatius, for instance, is known to have visited the church at Philippi. It is inconceivable that the matter did not come up for discussion! To overcome this difficulty scholars like Gore have suggested that before a localised episcopate emerged in the so-called presbyteral churches, there were itinerant apostolic figures, prophets and teachers (Clement seems to refer to *hegoumenoi* or 'rulers' who appointed the presbyters at Corinth; cf. Hebrews 13:7, 17). Such figures exercised oversight in these churches, even in relation to the council of presbyters. Gradually, as a president emerged in this council, the itinerant ministry of oversight became identified with that of the president. It is here that Gore's view of a primitive itinerant ministry of oversight coalesces with the views of Bishop Lightfoot and the Old Catholic scholar, Dr Langen, that the episcopate emerged from the need for a president in the council of presbyters so that what at first belonged to all was limited more and more to one.[9]

We have seen, thus, that there was a rich variety of ministries, lay and ordained, in the early church. We have seen, also, that significant distinctions were made between one kind of local ministry and another. The most dramatic division, however, seems to have been between the *local* and the *wider* ministries, such as those of apostle, prophet and teacher. These wider ministries contributed to the emergence of the historic episcopate as we have come to know it.

What shape should ministry have now?

Today, in the same way, we should expect to find a great diversity of ministries in the local Christian community. Particular gifts will be used for building up the body of Christ in a particular place. Other ministries will be required for outreach or for promoting good order in the church. Some churches will organise at least some of their ministries into ministry teams or leadership teams or groups for the exercise of one kind of ministry or another, such as healing. Other churches may be less organised, but there may nevertheless be a great flourishing of ministries. We should not be afraid of the variety and should maintain flexibility about organisation.

It is natural to expect that from such diversity there should emerge those who are to be the ordained ministers for the community. Their calling will not only be personal but communal. *Stranger in the Wings*, the Church of England report on what is now called Ordained Local Ministry (OLM), rightly emphasises the 'calling out by the church' of those who might not come forward in any other way.[10] Just as they are called out by the local community, their formation should take place in close conjunction with that community and with close attention to the significance of the local. It is here that an opportunity was, perhaps, missed when Non-Stipendiary Ministry (NSM) was first introduced. The paradigms for selection and training remained that of the stipendiary ministry and it is no surprise, therefore, to find that a significant number of NSMs transfer to the stipendiary category within a relatively short time of their ordination.

'Haven't you forgotten something?' some will ask. 'Where does the stipendiary ministry of the church fit into this grand plan?' Here the distinction between local and wider, settled and itinerant becomes relevant. To try to fit stipendiary clergy into a purely 'local' slot may not be the best use of resources available to us. They should be a precious resource whose deployment is strategic. More and more they will be seen as ministers of oversight: discerning gifts, facilitating training of all kinds, relating local Christian communities to the wider church. In all of this, they share the bishop's oversight. What had come to be held by one is again being shared.

What happens, then, to the unity of the presbyterate? It is true that in the Pastoral Letters and in Ignatius the *presbyterion* ('presbyterate') has a kind of homogeneity to it (1 Timothy 4:14; Ephesians 4:1; Trallians 3:1; Philadelphians 4:1). It must be asked, however, whether this admits of no diversity at all. The Pastorals and other early writings seem to distinguish between 'ruling' elders and others. They also show that there was a difference between those who held specific teaching and preaching responsibilities and the rest (e.g. 1 Timothy 5:17). Again, it is here that the lines converge between the wider and the local, between Gore and Lightfoot. The ruling, teaching elders are more and more like the apostolic delegates. Today also, we need presbyters whose ministry is primarily local and others who exercise a wider ministry. Each will have a dignity appropriate to their office. Vaguely collectivist and egalitarian notions should not distract us from the possibility of there being many different kinds of ordained ministry, just as there are different kinds of lay ministry.

In the early church, then, local presbyters and deacons were closely related to their context. This should be our ambition for today's local ministers too. They can be and ought to be committed to their locality in a way less and less possible for the stipendiary clergy. Again, in the early church, local ministers were to be found among a variety of ministries. This should be the case for us also, whether such variety finds expression in a team or in some other way.

Perhaps one other factor needs to be mentioned: John Drane and others have identified the need for tomorrow's pastors to be *missionary pastors*. In the context of Christendom, or of 'churched cultures', this was not necessary. The church's ministry was known to be open to everyone and people could and did avail themselves of it. Now things are increasingly different, and pastors who do not know how to deal with the unchurched can be disastrous for the church. It is important not only to take the opportunities that exist for rites of passage, for instance, but also to create new opportunities, such as celebrations and observances of anniversaries of births, marriages and even of bereavement. Focused visiting for preparation of couples getting married, parents wanting their children baptised and those who have been bereaved cannot, of course, be done simply by the pastors. The training of teams, their co-ordination and oversight, however, remains their job. Pastors need also to give a lead in imaginative programmes of evangelism, whether these are hospitality- and study-based, like Alpha or Emmaus, or based on pastoral care like prayer-visiting in the parish. Without this missionary dimension, professional pastors will simply preside over institutional decline. They may do a reasonably good job of this but the results will, nevertheless, be a dying church.[11]

We should not be so concerned about names and titles, as long as we are faithful to the patterns of ministry found in the Scriptures and in the life of the early church, and as long as we are addressing the needs of our locality. Such fidelity will recover for us local as well as wider ministries both rooted in the context *and* catholic in scope.

Many churches in the Anglican communion and beyond are engaged in a process of recovering for their own situation the variety and flexibility of ministry found in the New Testament and the early church. We need to learn from one another, reflecting on the developments taking place in the church worldwide. Such learning and reflection will surely bring about a transformation in our own perceptions of ministry, as well as those of our partners.

Pastors, presidents, priests?

We have seen ordained ministers as pastors, presidents and teachers. Are they also priests in some sense or other? It is often pointed out that the New Testament focus is on Jesus as the High Priest of the New Covenant (Hebrews 3:1; 8:1; 10:21) and on the whole people of God as a royal priesthood (1 Peter 2:9; Revelation 1:6; 5:10; 20:6). Gordon Kuhrt is surely right to point out that this is a *corporate* priesthood of the whole people and should not be taken to mean that individual believers have a priesthood to exercise apart from the whole body.[12] I am bound to say, though, that the sacrificial (and, therefore, priestly) language of Romans 12 does demand both a personal and an ecclesial reference: the presenting of bodies and transforming of minds must have to do with individual believers as well as the church of which they are part.

If, however, we are to consider how language of priesthood began to apply to ministers, we must look at the Eucharist. Tom Wright tells us that in instituting the Lord's Supper, Jesus was deliberately replacing the Temple cult with one where *he* was the victim to be remembered and the one of whom believers were to partake.[13] Already in 1 Corinthians 10:16–21, St Paul has used strongly sacrificial language of the Lord's Supper. The *Didache* reinforces this understanding with a reference to Malachi 1:11, and Ignatius speaks of the altar as the locus for the common celebration of the Eucharist (Ephesians 5:2; Philadelphians 4:1). As the recalling and making present of Christ's once-for-all sacrifice, in which believers participate through the sacramental sharing of bread and wine, it is easy to see how sacrificial language came to be used of the Eucharist. Eventually, of course, such language was abused when people thought they were somehow repeating again and again the sacrifice of Calvary. The changed significance of the elements, as the means through which the body of Christ and his blood are received, began to be thought of in crudely material terms. It is this the Anglican reformers opposed as overthrowing the nature of the sacrament (e.g. Article 28 of the Thirty-Nine Articles of Religion). They were concerned also to safeguard the unique nature of Christ's sacrifice, while teaching that we truly partake of Christ's body and blood and that the service of Holy Communion is 'our sacrifice of praise and thanksgiving'.

When the Eucharist came to be thought of as sacrifice, it was natural to think of those who presided at it as priests. In Ignatius (early second century) this is primarily the bishop but along with the presbyters and deacons. In Justin (mid-second century) it is the *proestos* or 'president', and in Cyprian and Origen (third century) it is the presbyter now referred to as priest (*hiereus* or *sacerdos*). In English the term 'priest' can be regarded as simply a contraction of the word 'presbyter' or it can have connotations of the Greek and Latin words meaning 'one who presides at the sacrifice of the people, who intercedes for the people and who absolves them in God's name'. In this sense also ordained ministers can be called priests, however we understand the sacrificial nature of the Eucharist, their prayer for the people and the declaration of forgiveness of sins (Matthew 16:19; 18:18; John 20:22–23). They are performing a doubly representative function: they represent Christ when they proclaim pardon and when they repeat the words and actions of the Lord of the Eucharist. They act on behalf of the people when they lead in the praying, the praising and the offering. In neither of these functions do they take away the right of believers to have direct access to God.[14]

It is often claimed that priestly language about Christian ministers was suggested to the early writers through their reading of the Older Testament. There is, no doubt, some truth in this claim. As the church came to be thought of as the people of God, it was inevitable that its ministry would be compared to that of the ancient people of God. In fact, some of the Fathers use explicitly levitical language about Christian priesthood.[15] There is, however, another, more eschatological, strand in the Older Testament that has influenced Christian thinking about priesthood.

Priestly service of the gospel of God

The last chapter of the book of Isaiah, that gospel in the Older Testament, is a high point in the Hebrew Bible. Here we find the great themes of Israel's election and destiny set within the context of God's universal purposes. We find that some, even from the Gentiles, have turned away from the heedlessness of the world and these are the 'survivors' who are sent both to declare God's good news to those who would listen and also to warn those who would persist in their ways. It is fitting, indeed, that a book beginning with a vision of all the peoples of the world streaming *to* Mount Zion (2:2–4) should end with the missionaries going *out* to bring the people into the sanctuary. But there is even more in this wonderful passage: the orthodox among the Jewish people, even after the exile, would have read verse 21 with great astonishment. Many commentators agree that this is a reference not only to the missionaries, themselves Gentiles, who will be sent out, but to the Gentiles whom they will gather. Some of these too will be priests and levites![16] It is clear that such people cannot belong to the hereditary, Aaronic, priesthood. Like the priesthood of Christ, their priesthood too must be unique. Later Christian thought was to refer to this as the priesthood of Melchizedek. Christ is High Priest according to the order of Melchizedek

(Hebrews 7; cf. Psalm 110:4), and those who share in his priesthood must also be priests according to the order of Melchizedek.

A passage such as Isaiah 66:18–24 must be in Paul's mind when he speaks of his apostolic ministry as a priesthood of the 'gospel of God' so that the offering of the Gentiles may be acceptable and sanctified by the Holy Spirit (Romans 15:16). The whole verse is redolent of priestly and sacrificial language. Of what, then, does this priesthood consist? For Paul, like the missionaries in Isaiah, it has to do with preaching and living the gospel. Paul makes it quite clear in the rest of the chapter that he has done precisely this throughout Western Asia and Southern Europe. It has to do with teaching and with deepening the faith of those who believe. Once again, we know that Paul was always alert to every possibility of deepening the faith of new believers, which means offering up the people God has entrusted to us so that they may be accepted and blessed by God. Isaiah says that such an offering will be as pure as the cereal offerings of the Israelites.[17]

CASE STUDY

Louis Massignon was a Melkite priest who spent nearly the whole of his life working among Muslims in Egypt. It was a difficult task and, from a human point of view, there was hardly any fruit. But every day, in the course of his prayers, he offered up to God the people to whom he had been called. He believed firmly that God would fulfil his purpose for them and that he was only a small part of God's plan. He called this offering tabdil, *his offering on their behalf.*

Romans 15:16 can, however, also be translated, 'Grace was given to me by God to be a priest of Christ Jesus to the Gentiles in the priestly service of the Gospel of God, *so that the worship which the Gentiles offer may be acceptable, sanctified by the Holy Spirit*.'[18] Again, as in Isaiah, it is the task of priests of the New Covenant to lead the people in worship. This does not, of course, mean that they do everything! It *does* mean making sure that everything is done and done with reasonable order. Paul, through his priestly ministry, makes it possible for the Gentiles to worship the one, true God. So too the Christian priest today enables people to bring offerings of thanks and praise, to join our unworthy and yet necessary sacrifices to the one, perfect sacrifice of Christ so that they may be acceptable to God (Romans 12:1–3; Philippians 3:10; Hebrews 13:13–15), helping us to draw near to the throne of grace knowing that Jesus Christ ever lives to plead for us (Romans 8:34; Hebrews 7:25; 10:19–22) and to offer up everything we have to God's service. We can add nothing to the saving uniqueness of Christ's atoning sacrifice but it is through him, and in the context of recalling his sacrifice, that we offer our own sacrifices to God (Hebrews 13:13–15).

Enabling the people to exercise their priesthood is costly. In a passage full of sacrificial imagery, St Paul tells the Philippian church that he is being poured out as a libation (or drink offering) on the sacrifice of *their* faith and generosity. The reference is clearly to his readiness for martyrdom (Philippians 2:17). Such a ministry needs to be sacrificial today also, whether in terms of financial reward, living where we would rather not live or being with people quite unlike us. In some parts of the world this still involves being ready for harassment, active persecution and even death.

This same eschatological thrust is maintained by the *Didache* when it refers to prophets as the 'high priests' of the Christian communities (13:3). True, the prophets are seen to have leadership in the celebration of the Eucharist (10:7), but the focus is on their ministry of bringing the good news, on teaching and on prophetic utterance consistent with a Christian style of life (chs 11 and 12). Elsewhere too, Christian ministers are called levites and priests because of their *ministry of the word*.[19] I shall quote the congregationalist C H Dodd in full as a kind of summing up of this difficult matter. Commenting on Romans 15:16 he says:

> It is in this truly spiritual sense that the Christian ministry is a priestly ministry. To deny its priestly character is to belittle its spiritual worth. Ministerial priesthood in this Pauline sense does not exclude the priesthood of all believers; for each individual Christian is called upon to dedicate his body as a living sacrifice. But the minister who brings men to Christ, and instructs and trains them in Christian living, is making that sacrifice possible, or helping to make it more real and complete. As the sacramental system of the church developed, the priesthood of the minister came to be more particularly connected with his administration of the sacrament of the Lord's Supper. Since that sacrament, as conceived by Paul, is a *participating* in the (mystical) *body of Christ*, it gives a fitting visible form to the *spiritual rite* of self-dedication, and the minister's part in it similarly gives visible form to his priestly relation to the church. It is when the self-offering of the church, in association with Christ's own sacrifice, is forgotten, or pushed into the background, that the abuses of sacerdotalism arise.[20]

We see thus that priestly language can justifiably be used for the ministry of preaching, presiding at worship and pastoral care of the people. This does not, of course, exclude other kinds of images and metaphors being used of the Christian minister.

The ministry of women

These days nearly everyone is agreed that women have a valuable ministry in the church, but there remains disagreement about the kind of ministry appropriate for them. Some would restrict such ministry to serving other women, some to the private sphere, and others, again, would allow public ministry but not presidency at worship. Some, at least, could see regular preaching as part of such presidency. Reluctance to allow women unimpeded access to ordained ministry is based on a host of theological, social and personal factors. Not all can be discussed here, but many who see the Christian ministry as organically related to the Israelite, point out that the Aaronic priesthood was limited to men. Then there are those who see as deeply significant Jesus' choice of twelve men as apostles, even though he had a number of prominent women disciples. St Paul's injunctions for women to be silent (1 Corinthians 14:34) and the Pastoral Epistles' prohibition on women teaching and having authority over men (1 Timothy 2:11–12) are determinative for some. It is said, moreover, that our Lord was quite able to challenge the social customs of his day, as was St Paul, and yet in this matter they did not break with tradition.

Naturally, each of these objections has been answered by those who favour women in the ordained ministry. The Aaronic priesthood, they tell us, was not only limited to men but was hereditary as well. This is something the Christian church has consistently refused to recognise as a basis for ministry. While the choice of the Twelve might have been determined by cultural factors, this involved not only their maleness but also their Jewishness and that they all came from Palestine. Again, neither of these other qualities has ever been a requirement for Christian ministry. As far as the Pauline passages are concerned, they have to be read in the light of clear teaching in 1 Corinthians 11 that women have a ministry of praying and prophesying in the assembly, even if Paul attempts to regulate this. Both this passage and the one about women being silent in church belong to a section on church order and it is thought unlikely that Paul would discuss *how* women should speak in church and absolutely forbid them to do so in the same section! Because of this, many commentators have seen this not as an imposition of silence but as a prohibition on the interruption of proceedings by asking questions that can better be asked at home, on gossip or talkativeness in church, or on needless enthusiasm in discussing prophetic messages. In addition, there are problems here with the text and its continuity that have led some to question even the authenticity of the verses under discussion.[21]

Admittedly, 1 Timothy 2:11–12 is a difficult passage seemingly rooted in an anthropology of the Fall. This sees women as subjected to men because of human sin (Genesis 3:16), a common view in Jewish circles at the time, but seemingly at variance with Paul's anthropology of a new creation in Christ. It has to be acknowledged that the 'household codes' in the Pauline corpus speak of wives submitting to their husbands (Ephesians 5:22; Colossians 3:18). This is in a domestic, rather than a church, context and follows the injunction to mutual submission (Ephesians 5:21). Indeed, it has been said that this mutuality is characteristic of the Christian household codes when compared to pagan ones.[22] In 1 Timothy this subordination of the woman to the man is extended to life in the church and is based on the order of creation and the consequences of sin!

And yet there are those who point out that the thrust of the teaching here is against women usurping authority and teaching in a domineering manner. If 'submission' is the biblical way, then such attitudes can never be justified.[23] It has also been suggested that the passage should be read in the light of the letter's attack on false teaching. Wealthy and influential women had been co-opted by these false teachers and were being used as 'spokespersons' to propagate error that included the forbidding of marriage and of bearing children. This quite particular situation is the context for the prohibition on women teaching with usurped authority.[24] Whoever teaches must teach in humility and in submission to the faith that has been received and needs to be handed on.

It has long been recognised, however, that the matter cannot be settled simply by producing proof-texts and arguing for or against them. The approach has to be wider than that, taking into account the whole sweep of the Bible and the direction in which it seems to be pointing. There are, first of all, the *theological considerations* relating to the nature of the incarnation itself. As Archbishop Robert Runcie pointed out in his correspondence with the Pope and Cardinal Willebrands of the then Vatican Secretariat for Promoting Christian Unity, the Eternal Word assumed flesh so that through the passion, resurrection and ascension of the incarnate Lord, the whole of humanity might be redeemed and taken up into the life of the triune Godhead. Behind this idea is the oft-quoted statement from Gregory of Nazianzus: 'What he did not assume, he did not heal.'[25] The humanity of the risen and ascended Lord is inclusive of male and female. This is the import of the *en Christo* ('in Christ') language of the New Testament and, more particularly, of passages such as Ephesians 2:6. It follows, therefore, that if ministers represent Christ, such representation would be more complete if their ranks included both men and women.[26]

Secondly, there are *anthropological considerations.* These should not depend on one or two texts but should try to determine a properly biblical view of the human condition and of its redemption in Christ. The proper place to start is at the beginning with Genesis 1, which gives an account of the creation of the first human beings: they are created together, for each other and in God's 'image' (*selem*). For the writer, the idea of the human being finds its full meaning not only in the male but in the male and the female together (vv. 26–27). Whatever value we give the later story of Eve being made from a rib or side of Adam's, or to the disruption in relations because of the Fall, we cannot lose sight of the fundamental truth that both man and woman are in the divine image and placed on earth as God's representatives to maintain and enforce the divine reign.[27] The New Testament speaks of the recreation of human beings in this image (which is Christ himself; e.g. Colossians 1:15). In Christ's incarnation, mission, suffering and rising from the dead God is restoring, renewing and, indeed, completing his task of making humanity in his own image. Those who are in Christ, who have put on the new humanity, are actualising God's purposes in their lives. It is in this context that the old distinctions between Jew and Greek, slave and free, male and female cease to matter, for we discover that we are 'one in Christ Jesus' (Galatians 3:28; Colossians 3:10–11). If such distinctions have ceased to matter in the church, can they still be made to matter in the ministry that represents the church as well as the Lord?

Finally, there are *practical considerations*: undeniably God has, throughout the course of history, given women gifts of leadership, of teaching and of celebrating. The culture of much of the Older Testament is patriarchal and, naturally, this brings men to the fore in leadership, including spiritual leadership. Even in such a situation, though, there are significant women who are leaders of the community. Miriam, the sister of Moses and Aaron, is described as a prophetess who leads the women in public praise of God at the time of the Exodus (Exodus 15:20–21). Then there is Deborah who not only judged Israel for some years but also led them in battle (Judges 4–5). During the monarchy, in the reign of the pious King Josiah, the prophetess Huldah interprets the implications of the newly found Book of the Law (Deuteronomy?) to the High Priest and the royal court. This leads to the great reformation and renewal of faith that characterises this reign (2 Kings 22:3 – 23:27; cf. 2 Chronicles 34:8 – 35:19). There are many other significant women in the biblical record. We need only think of Hannah, the mother of the prophet Samuel, whose song of praise is echoed in that other great song of praise, the *Magnificat* (1 Samuel 2:1–10; Luke 1:47–55). There is Ruth who becomes the ancestress of David and, therefore, of the Messiah, and Esther who provides leadership for her people at their time of need.

In the New Testament we must, of course, begin with Mary whose 'yes' to God is that of faith and makes the incarnation possible. She is the one who listens to God and ponders in her heart the great things God is doing (Luke 2:18, 51). Until recently in the Roman Catholic Church Mary was sometimes depicted as a priest because she brings forth the body of Christ and gives it to the world. Feminist theologians agree that this may be a different conception of priesthood from the male but that it is equally valid.[28] We cannot help but relate the church as the heavenly Jerusalem and the mother of the faithful to Mary the mother of Christ whose body the faithful are said to be (1 Corinthians 12:12; Galatians 4:26; Revelation 12). Nor should we forget Elizabeth in that 'supporting' role at the time of the Annunciation. She is the first to recognise Mary as *theotokos* or 'God-bearer', as she hails Mary as 'the mother of my Lord' (Luke 1:43; Matthew 1:23).

During the course of his public ministry, Jesus had many women disciples and St Luke tells us explicitly that some of them supported his ministry financially (Luke 8:2–3; cf. Matthew 27:55–56). Interestingly, the *Didascalia Apostolorum*, a third-century church order from Syria, cites these women as a justification for having women deacons. One of these, Mary Magdalene, the Pontifical Biblical Commission tells us, is called by tradition 'the apostle of the apostles'.[29] At the time of Pentecost, once again, we find the Twelve with Mary the mother of the Lord and other women.

Elisabeth Schüssler Fiorenza speaks of 'missionary couples' mentioned in the Acts of the Apostles and in the Pauline letters as apostolic.[30] Of these Andronicus and Junia are explicitly mentioned by Paul as being 'of note among the apostles' (Romans 16:7). He refers, moreover, in several places to women being his fellow-workers (Romans 16:3; Philippians 4:2), thus associating them with his apostolic task. In the subapostolic period we have accounts of women like Thecla who are commissioned by the apostles themselves to preach the word of God. There are other early accounts of women exercising a 'heroic' mission, sometimes in relation to their imprisonment, torture and martyrdom. Some of these women are still remembered: Felicity, Perpetua, Agatha, Lucy, Agnes, Cecilia and Anastasia, in addition to Thecla, who is commended by Jerome as an example to Christian women and is still greatly venerated in the East. The point is not so much whether any or all of these women existed or did all of the things with which they are credited, but the kinds of ministry it was thought possible for them to exercise.

As we have seen, the 'house churches' were an essential way of being church. It was often here that new Christians were discipled and brought to maturity in the faith. The New Testament specifically refers to the role of women in the leadership of these churches. Philippi was the first church planted on European soil. The account in the Acts of the Apostles shows us that, initially, this church was planted among women. The names of those who were Paul's fellow-workers here are almost all female: Lydia, Euodia, Syntyche. Along with Lydia, there are women like Nympha who are seen as leaders of the church in their homes (Colossians 4:15). However, another missionary couple, Prisca and Aquila, are mentioned again and again as leaders of the church in their home. We meet them first in Corinth, where they have arrived having been expelled from Rome by the emperor Claudius, then in Ephesus where they teach Apollos the faith 'more accurately', and, finally, in Rome again having returned there after the death of Claudius (Acts 18:1–4, 24–28; Romans 16:3–5; 1 Corinthians 16:19). It has often been noticed that Prisca (or Priscilla) is sometimes mentioned first. This may be a sign of her higher social standing or gift of leadership but it may also have to do with her importance in the early church. It is particularly important that in the Acts she is depicted as taking part in the discipling and teaching of a future leader of the church like Apollos.

Phoebe is called a deacon of the church at Cenchrea (near Corinth) but the term *diakonos* may mean simply 'minister' (Romans 16:1). The most intriguing thing about her is that she is referred to as the *prostatis* of many, including Paul himself. This term is usually translated 'protectress', 'patroness', or even 'help', but it *does* have connotations of a leading person and guardian. The male form, in both Jewish and pagan circles, has priestly overtones.

The Acts of the Apostles refer to women prophets (21:9) and in 1 Corinthians, we find the apostle attempting to regulate the activities of women prophets (11:5), though not to prevent them altogether. Bishop Gore tells us that just as there were 'prophetesses' in the apostolic church, so there continued to be well into the second and third centuries. He mentions Ammia of Philadelphia in particular. She was from the end of the second century and was claimed by the Montanists, though Eusebius affirms her orthodoxy. Gore's comments are significant because he derives the episcopal office from the ministries of apostolic figures as well as *prophets and teachers*.[31]

Of necessity we have concentrated on the biblical and early evidence but, of course, throughout the ages there have been women leaders of religious communities like Hilda of Whitby, who was highly influential at the Synod of Whitby (AD 664) – a synod that determined the course of the church in the British Isles for the next few centuries. Pioneering missionaries have not only proclaimed the gospel, but have taught the faith and led worship in countless situations.

Today also, as Archbishop Runcie says in his correspondence with the Vatican, churches that have admitted women to different ministries, including ordained ministries, have found this beneficial for the church as a whole.[32] The best argument for women in ministry is often the living, day-to-day example of women *engaged* in ministry, which challenges stereotypes and breaks down prejudice. Whatever decision churches make about the ordination of women, it must be in the light of their experience of women using the gifts the Holy Spirit has given them.

As we have seen, even within the Orthodox families of churches, both of the 'Eastern' type and the 'Oriental' type, great changes are afoot as far as women's ministry is concerned. There is considerable concern that women should be enabled to participate more fully in the life of the church and that certain ministries, like those of women deacons, should be revived.[33]

It has to be acknowledged, however, that church Fathers like Tertullian, Origen and Epiphanius were hostile to the ministry of women for two main reasons: they shared in the prevailing cultural view that women were inferior, and there was a deep-seated fear that allowing women to be priests would open the way for the church to be influenced by numerous pagan fertility cults, which celebrated not sacrifice but sexual fecundity as the foundation of religion.[34] The former view is no longer tenable and, while some women priests may see their ministry in terms of Christ giving birth to and nourishing the faithful, this is very far from fertility cults with their 'bestial monstrosities' and exploitation of women and men in cult prostitution! Whatever the justification for the fears of the Fathers, they can hardly serve as sufficient grounds for denying ordination to women now. It is true, of course, that men as well as women called to the ordained ministry need to understand it in the light of the church's teaching, even if they also make their own contribution to how this ministry is seen by their fellow-clergy and the rest of the faithful. Churches that ordain women should be clear that they are ordaining them to the apostolic ministry and are not inventing some novel form of ministry!

There remains concern, however, that the ordination of women will jeopardise and, perhaps, even extinguish ecumenical relations with some families of churches, such as the Roman Catholics, the Orthodox and the Oriental Orthodox. Against this, Dr George Carey, the Archbishop of Canterbury, when Bishop of Bath and Wells, said that such impairment of ecumenical fellowship has to be weighed against the damage to *koinonia* ('communion' or 'fellowship') by *excluding* women from the presbyterate and episcopate.[35]

If arguments from the Bible and from theological reflection lead us to affirm the possibility of ordained ministry for women, it is surely an injustice to deny them such a ministry solely to maintain or to promote unity? Authentic ecumenism is not at any cost but must include considerations of truth and justice as the different communities see them. Only then will there be true unity of heart, mind and spirit.

Labourers deserve their reward

In the days of Jesus' public ministry, it seems that his immediate disciples had left everything to follow him (Mark 10:28). Their needs were met through the donations of other followers (Luke 8:3), which were kept in a common purse (John 12:6; 13:29). This 'communism' seems to have continued in the very early church (Acts 2:44; 4:32; 5:1–11).[36] Even within the New Testament itself, however, we can detect changes as the Christian mission moves out into the gentile world. The repeated injunctions to practise hospitality, for example, suggest private means (Romans 12:13; Hebrews 13:2). In 1 Corinthians, Paul lays down guidance for the collection on Sunday (16:1–4). Again, this seems to mean that people had their own resources from which they were to set something aside for those in need. By the time of the Pastoral Letters, it has become necessary to admonish the rich not to be haughty but to be liberal and generous in sharing their worldly goods (1 Timothy 6:17–19). The *Didache*'s reference to the giving of the first-fruits implies the possession of private property and throughout the early writings there is an acknowledgement of private property, but also frequent warnings of its dangers and strong exhortations towards almsgiving, manumission of slaves, feeding and clothing the hungry and destitute and looking after those without a breadwinner in the family. Such was the extent of the church's charitable work that even hostile pagans had to admit its effectiveness.[37]

Against this background we must examine the question of remuneration for those in the full-time ministry of the church. In the Church of England the clergy are provided with 'a tied house', which is regarded as necessary for their job, and a stipend, which is seen not as reward but as a means of releasing someone to give their full attention to the ministry. The 1943 statement of the House of Bishops is often quoted to explain more fully the concept of a stipend:

> The stipends of the clergy have always, we imagine, been rightly regarded not as pay in the sense in which that word is understood in the world of industry today, not as a reward for services rendered, so that the more valuable the service in someone's judgement or the more hours worked the more should be the pay, but rather as a maintenance allowance to enable the priest to live without undue financial worry, to do his work effectively in the sphere to which he is called and if married to maintain his wife and bring up his family in accordance with a standard which might be described as that neither of poverty nor riches.

Some believe, however, that there is little scriptural or patristic support for this idea. It seems, rather, to have evolved from the need to correct the great disparity in incomes from land and tithes and is based on the assumption that clergy do similar work and have similar responsibilities and should thus be paid equally. One can imagine other ways of paying clergy that are more responsive to the prevailing market conditions and to the need for sufficient numbers of clergy. Such pay (whatever it is called) would be determined in relation to the responsibilities of particular tasks and in comparison with the remuneration offered for other professions.

It is often claimed that it is difficult to derive principles of clergy remuneration from the Scriptures and other early writings. Is this in fact the case or is the claim made only to allow people to ride their 'hobby-horses' on this issue? In St Luke's account of the sending out of the Seventy (or Seventy-two) in mission, there are specific directions about how the disciples are to behave (Luke 10:1–12). In verse 7, the principle is laid down clearly that the worker is worthy of the 'pay' (*misthos*), a term that can also mean 'reward'. In the parallel passage in Matthew 10:1–15 (which is, of course, about the sending out of the Twelve), the saying comes earlier with instructions about what to take for the journey and has the term *trophe*, meaning 'nourishment' or 'food', instead of Luke's *misthos*. Most scholars agree that the position of the saying in Luke is original and that the Matthean version is a reaction to any sense of worldly reward. It is interesting that the same verse has both the promise of reward and a warning against seeking excessive reward!

The Greek translation of the Older Testament, the Septuagint, tends to use *misthos* for the wage of a manual worker (Genesis 29:15; Exodus 2:9; Leviticus 19:13). There is criticism when payment is reduced (Deuteronomy 24:14) or withheld (Jeremiah 22:13) or beaten down (Malachi 3:5) or paid late (Deuteronomy 24:15). More specifically, *misthos* is used for the payment of Levitical services in the sanctuary (Numbers 18:31) and, negatively, for priests demanding a reward for their teaching (Micah 3:11). In these passages it translates a variety of Hebrew words.

It is difficult to say whether the statement 'The labourer deserves his wages' is an original saying of the Lord or whether he is appealing to a commonly accepted proverb. It is quoted in 1 Timothy 5:18 alongside Deuteronomy 25:4 and is regarded as Scripture. This suggests that it was seen as a saying of the Lord from an early date.

Both the quotation from Deuteronomy 25 and the Lord's command are in Paul's mind in 1 Corinthians 9. He begins this chapter by defending the genuineness of his apostleship. The three illustrations of soldier, vinedresser and shepherd, regarding the right of remuneration, are all used elsewhere in the New Testament of Christian ministers (2 Timothy 2:3–6; 1 Corinthians 3:6–7; John 21:15–17). Paul's teaching is that adequate remuneration is a right for those in ministry – even if he himself does not exercise this right.

1 Timothy 5:17, which comes just before the quotation from Scripture, tells us that the ruling elders should be considered worthy of double honour, especially those who labour in preaching and teaching. Here the principle of differentials is introduced. The word *proistemi* (to 'rule', 'preside' or 'direct') is used by St Paul for those who have a ministry of leadership and care in the local congregation (Romans 12:8; 1 Thessalonians 5:12). This is probably the meaning here. However, this term is also used by Justin Martyr, among other things, for presidency at the Eucharist. Thus the phrase could mean 'those presbyters who preside at the Eucharist, especially those who preach and teach'. It may be, however, that what is meant is leadership in general, but including leadership in worship, in preaching and in teaching.

The Greek term *time* could mean 'reverence' or 'respect' but, taking it along with the following verse with its quotations about reward, it strongly suggests 'honorarium' or compensation (a meaning well attested from secular usage).

The background may well be that of soldiers who receive 'double pay' for a job well done.

This differential of 'double honour' is taken a step further in the Apostolic Constitutions (a compendium of church law dating from the fourth century). It asserts, first of all, the principle that those who work in the church should be maintained by the church. It then sets out in detail the portions the different officers are to receive. At the same time it exhorts the ministers, especially bishops, to be moderate in their lifestyle. As we have seen, the *Didache* teaches, similarly, that ministers are to be supported from the first-fruits of members of the congregation, be they of harvest, of animals, of clothes or of money.

It seems, then, that Scripture and the early writings provide unambiguous support for the principle that the church should reward those in Christian ministry in a way that is commensurate with their responsibilities. The idea of differentials need not, however, be limited to the extent of responsibility in the church. It could also be related to the cost of living in a particular area or to the size of a person's family (after all, managing one's household well is one of the conditions for effective Christian ministry – 1 Timothy 3:4, 12).

There are, of course, those who are 'non-stipendiary' and, like St Paul, do not claim their right of being supported by the church. Ways need to be found for honouring and enabling such ministers, whether they are ordained or lay. 'Reward' is not always monetary. People can be rewarded in a number of ways that somehow recognise their service to the church and the community at large. Indeed, if the vision of ministry in this chapter is to be promoted, non-stipendiary ministers will have to be valued and recognised. Paying expenses properly, ensuring that there are regular educational and training opportunities, representation in the church's councils and adequate pastoral care are some of the ways in which such ministry can be honoured and enabled.

Reader: a valued ministry in the church

> It is fitting that after the scaffold he should approach the lectern. At the scaffold he stood before an unbelieving crowd; at the lectern he is before the believers. At the scaffold he was heard with surprise by the bystanders. He is now heard with joy by the brethren. (St Cyprian of Carthage, martyred AD 258, on why he had ordained a reader without consulting the church)

Confessing the faith has long been associated with the ministry of reading, and those who bear witness to the faith in the world outside are most effective as ministers inside the church. Conversely, their ministry in church equips them and others to bear witness in the world. It is this mutuality of ministry in church and world that has given vigour to the office of Reader down the ages.

There are now more Readers in the Church of England than stipendiary clergy. In the same way there are lay ministers, of one kind or another, in other denominations. The office and work of a Reader is rooted in the New Testament. The reading of apostolic letters and of prophecy was clearly an important task in the early assemblies (Colossians 4:16; Revelation 1:3). In his First Apology, Justin refers explicitly to the Reader in the context of the Sunday assembly and celebration of the Lord's Supper. In some parts of the church Readers were appointed with the laying on of hands and Cyprian, certainly, refers to this as 'ordination' (letter 38). Hippolytus, though, provides for a simple enrolment with the giving of the Bible.[38] In the Eastern churches the Reader (or Lector) is often also a deacon. In the Roman Catholic Church, Readers or Lectors are ministers who read the Scriptures (except the Gospel) and have other duties in the liturgy.

Although there was an attempt by Archbishop Parker soon after the Reformation to revive the office of Reader, it was revived in the Church of England only in the nineteenth century.[39] The duties of Readers include the taking of non-eucharistic services, such as Matins and Evensong, assisting in the distribution of Holy Communion, preaching, the instruction of children and assisting the incumbent in such pastoral work as the bishop may direct. Some now have permission to officiate at funerals. Women were first admitted in 1969 and there are now several thousand women Readers.

In the early days Readers could not preach if clergy were present and could not use the pulpit when they did preach! All that has changed now. Readers are often people who are very able in their own professions and, sometimes, they have the expertise to relate issues arising from their discipline to the Christian faith. Their teaching and preaching ministry is a distinctive and valuable complement to the ministry of clergy. In a visible way they model the ministry of lay people. We thank God for the revival of this ministry.

We have seen, then, how in a changing church we require a ministry that is faithful to Christian origins, properly understood, and flexible in a world where change is continuous. God gives us the gifts we need, which we are to discern and use for the building up of the church and for the glory of the Lord of the church.

7. One So That the World May Believe

CASE STUDY

The Church of England has a primary school on a new housing estate. From the beginning there has been a desire to have a single church on the estate, worshipping in the school hall. This has now begun to happen and there are people from Anglican, Baptist, United Reformed and other backgrounds coming along on a Sunday morning. Should the congregation be allowed to develop its own life entirely independently, or should the different churches provide some guidelines about how the new congregation is to relate to them? Should there be distinctive styles of worship, turn by turn, with everyone welcome to join to the extent they are able, or should the ministers and congregation aim for a style common to all? It is early days and yet church leaders and members of the congregation are already having to grapple with quite complex questions about their identity and relationship with the wider church and the world around them.

One of the most welcome features of the last century was the ways in which divided Christians and churches began to discover one another and to talk to one another. One of the main reasons for this was missionary: Christians realised that they could not be effective in mission if they remained divided and also that their division was an impediment to mission. When Dr Ambedkar, the leader of the Untouchables in India, was considering their conversion *en bloc* to Christianity, he asked Bishop Azariah of Dornakal whether such converts would be united in a single church and whether there would still be caste prejudice in such a church. It is said that Azariah was greatly disturbed and embarrassed by these questions. He had been an active participant at the Edinburgh Missionary Conference in 1910 (generally regarded as a watershed in the ecumenical movement) but Ambedkar made him redouble his efforts for church unity in India.[1]

Some global developments

The coming into being of the Church of South India in 1947 and of the Churches of North India, Pakistan and Bangladesh in 1970 was the fruit of labours like those of Bishop Azariah. The unity was partial, though, and while there have been unity schemes in plenty, this model of organic union has not been pursued anywhere else. As Lakdasa de Mel, the last Anglican Metropolitan of India, said at the 1968 Lambeth Conference, the worldwide church seemed to want unity 'down to the last Indian'. In other words, it is all right for them but it is not for us.

The entry of the Roman Catholic Church into the ecumenical movement, as a result of Pope John's 'opening of the windows' and *aggiornamento*, which looked to the renewal of the church and a fresh presentation of the ancient faith, made a huge impact on the world. The Second Vatican Council he had summoned, through its *Decree on Ecumenism*, changed radically the Roman Catholic Church's attitude to other Christians. Both the Decree and the *Constitution on the Church*, while continuing to teach that the church of Christ 'subsists' in the Roman Catholic Church, acknowledge also that many of the elements of that church exist elsewhere to build up and give life to Christian communities separated from the Roman Catholic Church.[2] The recognition of the extent to which these elements are present in other communities varies from one to the other. It is clear that the Council could recognise much more in common with the Orthodox churches than it could with the churches of the Reformation. It is interesting, in this connection, that the Anglican communion is mentioned especially as retaining 'elements of catholic faith and order' (*fidem et structuram ecclesiasticam*). It is, perhaps, for this reason that Pope Paul VI was able to refer to it as 'an ever-beloved sister'. We have seen, however, that the recognition of a common baptism and even the ecclesiality of other churches has not led to greater eucharistic sharing. In spite of Pope John Paul's eirenic letter *Ut Unum Sint*, there has been a hardening of attitudes towards other Christians. This is shown especially in the declaration *Dominus Iesus*, but is apparent also in other documents produced by the Vatican's Congregation for the Doctrine of the Faith (the successor to the Holy Office) and in some local teaching material.[3]

While the Roman Catholic Church has joined local and regional councils of churches in many parts of the world, sometimes helping to restructure them, it has cited 'ecclesiological reasons' for its reluctance in joining the World

Council of Churches. Perhaps it fears, like the Orthodox who *are* members, the radical–liberal agenda of the staff in Geneva. The World Council itself does not appear too keen for the Roman Catholics to join, even if they have been long-standing members of some of its most important bodies, like the Faith and Order Commission. Perhaps some are apprehensive of the entry of such a large church and what that would do to the balance of the WCC. In Britain and Ireland the structure of the ecumenical instruments had to be rethought so that the Roman Catholic Church could participate in them. Something similar is needed at the worldwide level. Instead of setting up parallel structures, as some have proposed, we need to ask 'What structures will enable the Roman Catholic Church to participate fully in the ecumenical movement at world level?' Its absence from the present structures seriously hinders the work and witness of the church as a whole. This is true also of the absence of some evangelical and Pentecostal churches. Again, the experience in Britain and Ireland confirms that asking fundamental questions about the nature of the ecumenical movement and the instruments needed to sustain it often secures the participation of at least some of these churches.[4]

The importance of the local

Most Christians, of course, experience unity at the local level, if they experience it at all. This may be through 'Churches Together', local 'covenant' schemes, ecumenical study groups or events like the Good Friday procession and act of worship and witness. The most sustained and profound experiences, however, are often in the context of a

Local Ecumenical Partnership (LEP). These are of many different kinds but, typically, they involve local congregations, along with the sponsoring denominations and the regional ecumenical body, entering into an agreement regarding the sharing not only of buildings but of life together. There may be some sharing of ministry, joint worship from time to time and encouragement to attend the worship of other participating denominations, as appropriate. After the failure of the Anglican–Methodist scheme, some had put forward the uniting of local churches as a first step in the emergence of a nationally united church.[5] Those LEPs with such a vision naturally see themselves as a vanguard and have developed a life that emphasises common worship, common ministry and common membership. As a nationally united church has failed to emerge, these LEPs often appear as 'third churches' to their parent denominations, which, sometimes, do not know how to relate to them. In the absence of a united church, surely LEPs should be communities where the *distinctives* of each tradition are maintained so that they can be shared, as far as possible, with the other partners? This does not rule out some common worship and some shared ministry, nor does it rule out a common mission in the wider community. In the present situation, however, 'mish-mash' ecumenism in LEPs will only produce the 'lowest common denominator' in worship and, more seriously, rootless local Christian communities that will have hardly a point of reference outside themselves.

In addition to the 'older' kind of ecumenism, there is some evidence of new kinds of interchurch co-operation. 'Churches Together' nowadays often include churches from a very wide range, including Pentecostal and renewal-minded churches. There are also other interdenominational fellowships that include churches of this kind. The focus here is not so much on organic or 'visible' unity, even at the local level, but a 'unity in the Spirit'. This can take the form of prayer and praise meetings, clergy fraternals and joint mission.

CASE STUDY

In an urban area, on Wednesdays at lunchtime there is a packed meeting of prayer and praise in an Anglican–United Reformed Church LEP building. Most of the energy for this does not, however, come from the hosts, but from churches of all kinds in the neighbourhood. The meeting, which is of course restricted to the lunch hour, has nevertheless been the launching pad for a host of mission initiatives, including a comprehensively ecumenical mission to the city, the sponsoring of evangelists from other parts of the world to visit the area, and a huge millennium event in the local football ground. Is this the new kind of ecumenism we shall see in the future?

I am delighted with this kind of ecumenism and give it my support, but I am left with a nagging feeling that the 'older' kind also had something of value that we should not forget. It is more difficult to put into words what that is but an attempt must be made.

Beyond respect and co-operation?

Many Christians now understand that God has blessed and made fruitful the ministry and outreach of churches other than their own. Do we need, however, to get further than this, further than occasional contact and co-operation over some pressing issue? The New Delhi Assembly of the WCC in 1961 produced a well-known statement on the church's unity that spoke of the unity of all in each place and also of these being in fellowship or communion with the whole church in all places and in all ages. This suggests more than just mutual respect. It implies a deep sharing in life around the word and in the sacraments. It demands that there should not only be a mutual recognition of ministries but interchangeability. It requires structures for consultation, common decision-making and accountability.

It should be said immediately that this does *not* mean uniformity, whether locally, nationally or globally. The kind of unity we are talking about is certainly more than a 'federal' arrangement to which churches can belong. Organic language is both appropriate and biblical in this context – but the body is, at the same time, closely interrelated and highly differentiated. It is quite proper, then, to speak of 'unity in reconciled diversity'. Each of those words is important though: we must work at unity in faith and life, not just agree to differ. The diversity must be within the bounds of that which makes our unity possible and there must be a real convergence in our understanding of the place of Scripture in the church, of the necessity of continuity with the church down the ages, of a ministry recognised everywhere and by all. It has often been pointed out that many of the issues *between* churches regarding the faith 'once delivered to the saints' and how it relates to change, the question of authority, where it is located and how it is exercised and the limits of diversity, are also issues *within* churches. They need to be addressed ecumenically as well as denominationally in terms of all that we have said in relation to the receiving of Scripture and Tradition in every age and every place and the possibility of development in the church's understanding of Scripture and Tradition.

Where there has been disagreement about the nature of the ordained ministry or questions about its continuity or both, this will have to be sorted out in the context of a united but diverse church. As is well known, in the Church of South India this situation was addressed by accepting the ministries of all the uniting churches without any further act *and* by making provision that future ordinations would be by bishops in historic succession. The recently inaugurated concordat between the Episcopal Church in the USA and the Evangelical Lutheran Church of America is similar to the South India model in that there is immediate recognition and sharing of presbyteral ministry. It is different in that the concordat does not begin with all bishops in the historic episcopate but it pledges to work towards such a situation.[6]

Because of the controversy caused by the South India Scheme, particularly in the Anglican communion, the later North India and Pakistan Scheme provided for a reconciled ministry in the united church from the outset. In fact, the ministries were reconciled within the context of the united church's inauguration. This was important because it signalled that any one of the uniting churches was not to be seen as 'conferring' orders on the ministers of another but, rather, the whole church, including ministers, for the sake of the gospel, was asking God to commission all ministers, through the *mutual* laying on of hands and prayer, for ministry in the new context created by the union.[7] The unsuccessful Welsh Plan followed North India and Pakistan in this respect.[8]

The reconciliation of churches will have to involve the reconciliation of ministries in some form, especially in churches that place a high value on the continuity of ministry down the ages. As has been pointed out, this need not be seen as the 're-ordination' of the ministers of the one by those of the other. It can, rather, be seen as a commissioning for ministry in a new context that draws on the resources and heritage of all the uniting traditions and seeks to place the uniting church in the context of continuity.

How churches are changing

Ecumenical dialogue and schemes of union are slowly changing the structure of and the ways in which communions of churches have understood themselves. If we take the Anglican communion as an example, it has, in the past, seen its identity as rooted in the *Ecclesia Anglicana*, the historic Church of England, particularly in the shapes it has taken since the Reformation. As Anglicanism has spread worldwide, it has continued to look to England for doctrine, liturgy and even spirituality. True, this is changing rapidly: as the different provinces grow in maturity, they are beginning to drink from their own wells, developing their life and witness in ways suited to their cultures and contexts. Our own diocesan link with the Diocese of Harare has shown us how this is happening in one particular area. This is not all, however: during the course of the last century, the Church of England, and the Anglican communion as a whole, has come to develop special relationships with churches of non-Anglican origin.

Already in the nineteenth century the Church Missionary Society's 'Mission of Help' to the ancient churches of India resulted, ultimately, in the emergence of the Mar Thoma Syrian Church, which came eventually to be 'in communion' with several Anglican provinces, including the Church of England. The Bonn Agreement of 1931 provides the basis for 'intercommunion' between the Old Catholic churches and the churches of the Anglican communion. The Old Catholics are a family of churches that have separated from the Roman Catholic Church at different times and over various issues, including that of papal infallibility. They are found in continental Europe and North America. The Lusitanian Church of Portugal, which was in communion with Anglicans on the same basis as the Old Catholics, is now a full member of the Anglican communion. The Philippines Independent Catholic Church, which arose out of the war of independence against Spanish rule, is also in communion on the same basis as the Old Catholics. As we have seen, since the 1940s Anglicans have united with Christians of other traditions in the South Asian subcontinent. These churches are now in 'full communion' with the different provinces of the Anglican communion and are fully represented in Anglican bodies such as the Lambeth Conference, the Meeting of Primates or Heads of Churches and the Anglican Consultative Council. By approving the Porvoo Declaration, the Anglican churches in Britain and Ireland have entered into 'communion' with the Lutheran churches of Scandinavia and the Baltic area.[9] This last was anticipated in the 'special relations' the Church of England had, for example, with the church of Sweden. Once again, as a diocese, we have been able to establish church and civic links with Estonia. Part of the impetus for this has undoubtedly come from Porvoo. The new relationship between the Episcopal Church in the USA and the Lutherans there will also affect the ways in which the Anglican communion understands itself.

The *Called to Be One* process, which sought to set the agenda for Christian unity in these islands for the new millennium, pointed out that in the older ecumenical agreements between Anglicans and other churches, as well as those involving other worldwide denominations, no provision was made for mutual consultation and decision-making.[10] These days, however, such a need is felt actively as churches grapple with new issues and live in rapidly changing societies. Because the united churches of South Asia are members of all the various instruments of communion, in theory, at any rate, they participate in all Anglican consultation and decision-making. The Porvoo Declaration explicitly provides for 'appropriate forms of collegial and conciliar consultation on significant matters of faith and order, life and work'. There is now also an international co-ordinating group with the Old Catholics and new structures in Europe for common mission and consultation among the different churches in communion.

All of this means that the Anglican communion is changing subtly from being a family of churches rooted in a particular tradition to being part of a wider family of churches, from different ecclesial traditions, each of which recognises the apostolic faith in the others. No one has as yet, however, successfully taken up Archbishop Runcie's challenge to find a name for this emerging reality – 'wider episcopal fellowship' was tried but found wanting. Such developments in the Anglican communion are paralleled, no doubt, in other parts of the worldwide church. Nor can they be simply dismissed as 'pan-protestant'. In the case of Porvoo, for instance, the greatest care was taken that the very elements of 'catholic faith and order' recognised in the Anglican communion by the Second Vatican Council were not compromised.

What is *koinonia* for?

It is basic to our faith that the love that binds the persons of the blessed Trinity together flows over into the creation and redemption of the world. The *koinonia* or fellowship of the church too cannot be for its own sake. It must be, as St Paul has put it, 'partnership for the sake of the gospel' (Philippians 1:5; my translation). The fundamental orientation in this passage is *outwards* to the world, not *inwards* towards a contemplation of internal relations in the church.[11] Konrad Raiser, the General Secretary of the World Council of Churches, is right to remind us that God's mission is directed at the whole *oikoumene* (the 'inhabited world').[12] Today this term cannot be understood to mean only humanity. It must include all of God's creatures – all that is the object of divine concern and of human stewardship.

Still less can the term stand for the church, even the worldwide church. The church is certainly a special instrument in the fulfilling of God's purposes (Ephesians 3:9–11) and it has a place in the new order that God is bringing about (Revelation 21 and 22). But it cannot be identified with that order, nor does it exhaust all that God is doing in creation.

God is working out his purposes in many and diverse ways. This is why it is right to emphasise our solidarity with all those struggling to become what they were intended to be in the purpose of God. Dialogue is indeed the basis for mission. The church needs to *listen* to men and women as they share their vision with us and speak of their spiritual quest. Christians need to develop *sympathy* for the spiritual aspirations of others and solidarity with them in their struggle. But this is not *all* of dialogue. In the course of dialogue, if gospel integrity is to be maintained, it is also necessary to relate people's struggles and aspirations to God's eternal purpose revealed in Jesus Christ (Ephesians 3:11). In other words, dialogue is an occasion for listening and sympathy, but it is also an opportunity for sensitive and appropriate *witness* to the gospel.

Christians can never forget that the overflowing divine love is seen most perfectly in the figure of the Suffering Servant, the one whose lordship was defined by his service. An important aspect of our discipleship and fellowship will be, therefore, to serve one another and the world around us (John 13:14–16; Romans 12; Galatians 6:10; Hebrews 13:1–6). In an unequal world, the churches also will inevitably have unequal resources for their service and action in the world. The sharing of resources is an important aspect of fellowship in the New Testament. Every church should have what it needs for its mission so that 'there will be equality' (2 Corinthians 8:14). Are we sharing resources equitably at every level of our life together?[13] Within the churches, and in different parts of the world, some are called for particular kinds of service. These may be religious communities, mission societies or development agencies like Tearfund or

Christian Aid. Are our churches in full and effective partnership with such bodies 'for the sake of the gospel'? Is there mutual trust, transparency and accountability in these relationships? Do we use the skills and resources available in such voluntary movements for the building up of the church and for mission?

Again and again, we are reminded of Jesus' High Priestly prayer that we may be one, even as he and the Father are one (John 17:11). But we need always to keep the missionary challenge of this prayer before us: 'that they may all be one . . . *so that the world may believe*' (John 17:21 RSV, my italics). The deepening and strengthening of our *koinonia* is for the sake of the divine mission to the world.

8. Rendering to Caesar

CASE STUDY

Terry has serious learning difficulties and lives in a home run by a private firm on behalf of the health authorities. He attends church regularly and, recently, expressed his desire to be confirmed. The staff co-operated with those who were preparing him for confirmation – until a date for it was announced. Suddenly everything had to be referred to an 'ethics committee'. Terry's wishes seemed irrelevant. When asked what would have been done in the case of Muslims, Hindus or Jews, the reply was that these were religious communities with 'rights'!

In the end, Terry was confirmed and it was a joyful occasion, but the events raised all sorts of questions: Do public institutions in this country have an obligation to meet the spiritual needs of those whom they serve? Can it be assumed that the churches (including the established church) will behave ethically in their ministry to people who are vulnerable? What role will the church play in the meeting of spiritual need among those in residential care?

Behind these are wider questions about the relationship of the church to the state. Should the formal link continue? Is it to the church's advantage? How should we be preparing for change? Is it possible to continue with a Christian basis for pastoral care in hospitals, prisons and universities, while remaining open to care by representatives of other faiths for their own people?

What does the Bible say?

During its wanderings and in the early period of the settlement, Israel was a near-theocracy ruled by prophetic figures like Moses and, later on, Joshua. For a time, judges ruled Israel, but on the insistence of the people (1 Samuel 8:4f), they were provided with a king, even though Samuel warned them that, as in the other nations, a king would quickly turn into an oppressor.

It was David who turned this somewhat concessionary monarchy into 'sacral kingship'. He modelled himself on the lines of the ancient Jebusite kings, whose kingship dated back to the time of Abraham and Melchizedek (Genesis 14:17f) and who functioned as both priests and kings. The presence of the prophets, however, often prevented the monarchy from becoming absolute. This is shown, for example, in the story of Nathan and David (2 Samuel 12:1–15), of Elijah and Ahab (1 Kings 18) and of Amos and Amaziah (Amos 7:10–17). The post-exilic failure to restore the line of David, and the reality of foreign rule, led to the intensification of the expectations regarding the Messiah, the awaited king of the line of David, who would restore past glories to the people of Israel. In this 'ideal' king of the Psalms and some of the prophets, in the one who was to be like Moses leading the people to freedom, and in the figure of the Suffering Servant of God, such expectations were invested.

The New Testament sees these expectations realised in the person and work of Jesus Christ who is himself the kingdom (Luke 17:21), though a kingdom of a very different kind from those of the petty rulers of the time, or even of the Roman Empire. The kingdom of God is revealed in Jesus and will come in fullness when God's purposes, as disclosed in Jesus, are fulfilled for the whole world. Such an end will truly be Jesus-shaped and God's kingly rule, inaugurated in Jesus and experienced in the life of the church, will become universal. Something like this is meant when the church prays *Maranatha* for the coming of the Lord (1 Corinthians 16:22; Revelation 22:20; *Didache* 10:6). In the meantime, the church, living between the ages, has the twofold task of acknowledging the rightful place of earthly rulers with their God-given responsibilities (Romans 13; 1 Peter 2:11–17), and declaring that it cannot allow Caesar to usurp what belongs to God: 'We must obey God rather than men' (Acts 5:29, RSV). In the New Testament there is also the sense that authorities can abuse their position and demand obedience, which the Christian must refuse because it means worshipping false gods of power, technology and money (Revelation 13).

The early years

The first three centuries of the Christian era can be characterised as an attempt to engage with the authorities by giving them an account of what Christians believed, assuring them that Christians were no threat to the state and arguing that there were witnesses to Christian belief in the traditions already existing in the ancient world. The literary genre of the so-called apologies, whether of Justin, Tertullian or Cyprian, is one that addresses itself to rulers in the hope that such an exercise will make life easier for Christians.[1] At the same time, we know that Christians were always viewed with suspicion as 'atheists' who were subverting the religious basis of the Empire (Roman or Persian) or that of civic polity (e.g. Acts 19:21–41). When active persecution broke out it was sometimes because they were suspected of heinous practices such as cannibalism and incest or because they refused to sacrifice to the gods and the genius of the emperor. There is also some evidence that at times their 'misdeeds' were so taken for granted that they were persecuted 'for the name alone' (*propter ipsum nomen*): they were asked three times if they were followers of Christ and if they persisted in saying that they were, their execution quickly followed.[2] In spite of this, Christians were always declaring their loyalty to the state and their willingness to give 'honour where honour was due'.

Constantine and all that

The first Edict of Toleration in the Roman Empire, issued by the dying Galerius, as well as Constantine and Licinius, was a rather grudging decision to allow Christians to exist and was somewhat less generous than the equivalent treaty in Persia, the Edict of Yazdgard, promulgated a hundred years later.[3] The Edict of Milan improved matters somewhat but it must be noted that throughout his reign Constantine was concerned to strike a balance between his instinctive sympathy for Christianity and his desire to conciliate the pagans.

In spite of this, however, the link between church and state grew stronger as, on the one hand, the church was given various privileges and, on the other, people took to appealing to the emperor for the settlement of church disputes. Constantine's calling of the Council of Nicaea and his presidency of it (even though as yet he was unbaptised!) set the seal on the Byzantine notion of sovereigns as rulers of both church and state – a notion that later served as a counterpoint to temporal papal claims.[4] In the East itself, monasticism arose as a conscious rejection of such 'worldly' Christianity. Even theological divisions had an underlay of hostility to Byzantium. In part, at least, the rise of Islam, and the welcome it received in some countries, can be explained by such hostilities.

The barbarian invasions left the Eastern Empire on its own and, somewhat paradoxically, had the effect of enhancing the authority of the Bishop of Rome in the West. In due course, however, when national monarchies began to emerge in the West, the monarchs often looked to the monarchy of David in ancient Israel and to the Byzantine model for inspiration. Throughout the Middle Ages there was a struggle between the temporal claims of the papacy, on the one hand, and, on the other, the attempts by European monarchs to gain control of the church within their territories. The so-called investiture controversy, where the monarchs demanded that newly appointed bishops should pay them homage and receive their pastoral staff and ring from the sovereign, was resolved only when it was agreed that the Crown should continue to receive homage and have a say in the appointment of bishops but should not insist on 'investing' the new bishop with staff and ring. Thomas à Becket may have won in his struggle against Henry II regarding the so-called benefit of clergy; that is, the exemption of clergy from trial in secular courts. (In spite of his murder by barons loyal to the king, the 'benefit' remained in force until the nineteenth century.) In wider terms, however, the position of the monarchs continued to gain strength throughout the Middle Ages. The invitation to bishops (as well as to abbots and priors of monastic houses) to sit in the *Witan*, or Anglo-Saxon parliament, and the confirmation of this practice from the time of the Model Parliament (1295), was based on the recognition that they were considerable landowners. They were, however, also extremely influential as advisers and counsellors to the king and could be, as we have seen, very dangerous enemies. It was necessary, therefore, to control their activities and to have them where they could be seen.[5]

Church and state in England

The establishment of the Church of England, which was given definite form under the reigns of Henry VIII and Elizabeth I, stems from these mediaeval developments, many of which were common to Europe as a whole. While the age-old and universal system of elections of bishops was upheld in the continuing role of the cathedral chapters, the monarch's role was strengthened from simply making sure that an acceptable candidate was elected to one where the monarch nominated the person to be elected and compelled the chapter to elect him! Since that time, the church has gained a significant say in who is nominated in the first place, and also, from the point of view of the Crown, the penalties against a recalcitrant chapter have been removed.

The most recent report on reforming the system of appointing diocesan bishops in the Church of England recognises that the Church recommends names to the Prime Minister who then chooses the one to be nominated by the Crown. The person nominated still needs the consent of the local church, whether through election by a cathedral chapter (or college of Canons as they are now called) or in some other way. Such a process has then to be confirmed, on behalf of the whole Church, by the Metropolitan or Archbishop of the province, who also provides the new bishop with the mission that has to be fulfilled in the diocese and the wider church.[6] Until relatively recent times, however, royal patronage, whether exercised directly by the Crown or by ministers, has often determined the nature of the episcopate as a body, its policies and priorities. There is no doubt that at times the Crown's motives were entirely laudable while at other times they were not.[7]

Whatever the form of its establishment, the Church of England has always seen its work in terms of a 'catholic mission to the nation'. Such a comprehensive vision has involved not only a commitment to be present in every local community and to provide Christian ministry in it but also to be concerned with the larger issues of state. Many have seen both ends of the commitment safeguarded by the formal relationship between church and state. If the state wants to hear the voice of the church in its Councils, then, it is asserted, the church should be willing to provide such a voice, as long as it sees this as an opportunity not for privilege but for service. Such a place can only be accepted without compromising the gospel, of which the church is steward, and by understanding itself as particularly an advocate of those who have no voice in the corridors of power: the poor, those on the margins of society, the refugees and the vulnerable.[8]

Naturally, such an arrangement cannot be one-sided: if the church is to have a voice in the affairs of the nation, it is only fair that the nation should have some voice in the affairs of the church. Methods of appointment to various offices in the church and the role of Parliament in having a final say in certain kinds of church legislation (excepting doctrine and worship) have been some of the ways in which the nation's participation has been ensured. Of course, the nature of establishment has changed continuously down the ages and, no doubt, will continue to change in the future. Also, there are different kinds of establishment: that of the Church of Scotland, for example, gives a lesser role to the state while some models in the European continent may give a greater role. It is true, also, that even if a church is disestablished, it may nevertheless remain a *national* church, with a commitment to the whole nation and to every community within it. The Church of England, for example, already pays for the bulk of its programme of maintenance and mission and this would continue in a new situation. The Roman Catholic Church in France, on the other hand, as the national church of France and guardian of much of the country's built heritage, continues to receive assistance in the maintenance of its buildings, even though it has been strictly separate from the state since the time of the French Revolution.[9]

Changing Britain

One of the changes that has occurred already has to do with an increasing awareness of Britain (and, indeed, the West generally) as a multicultural and multifaith society. Some of this has undoubtedly to do with an increasing presence of people of faiths other than Christianity, but it also has to do with a postmodern mindset where people pick 'n' mix their own spirituality, worldview and moral commitment. To those who wish to banish the influence of religion from the public sphere, this is a heaven-sent opportunity to claim that, because of these new circumstances, it is no longer appropriate for a particular church to be established.

Clearly those who most want such an outcome are the 'secularisers' who believe that public discussion should not be 'informed' by any one tradition, but that its rules should be purely formal. Out of disagreement may emerge a consensus that, likely as not, will be utilitarian in outlook and heavily dependent on the shifting sands of public opinion. As a matter of fact, however, even today much public discourse is influenced by values that stem from the Christian tradition, whether this is recognised or not.

It has to be said straight away that people of other churches and of other faiths are generally not the ones demanding disestablishment. They see the value of the state recognising the spiritual in some form. They are aware also of the enormous contribution made by the Judaeo-Christian tradition (however clumsy that term might be) to the polity, law and civic structures of this society. They want to make their own contribution but not at the expense of what is there already. For its part the Church of England has seen itself as protecting the legitimate interests of other churches and other faith communities. This was seen most dramatically in the debates on education in the 1980s where bishops in the House of Lords took the lead in making sure that there was sufficient provision for the teaching of non-Christian faiths in the national curriculum. In addition to speaking *on behalf of* other communities, the church has also supported their enfranchisement so that they could speak *for* themselves. The introduction of members of other churches and faith communities into the House of Lords brings to fulfilment a desire of the church for many years. Increasingly, the Church of England has made room for other churches and faith communities in chaplaincy work in universities, prisons and civic bodies, while seeking to retain a Christian basis for such services.

Naturally, all of this has to be done in a way that does not compromise the church's message or mission. It *can* be done, however, and *is* being done. In such circumstances, the church should see itself as the guardian of the spiritual and moral tradition that has provided the political, legal and intellectual framework for the nation's life. Such an attitude is quite compatible with making sure that others are able to contribute within this overall and developing framework.[10]

What a coronation should be

The next coronation may well be a litmus test of the way the country wishes to go. Will it be a 'multifaith inauguration' as some have suggested, or will it remain a distinctively Christian rite to which others, nevertheless, are invited?

The coronation rite in this country has a very long history, going back to before the Norman Conquest, and has changed little down the centuries. Its setting within the Eucharist reminds us that it is essentially a Christian event during which the monarch is consecrated for service, *anointed* as a sign of God's enabling and given a *Bible* to show from where his or her authority derives. The explicitly Christian character of the service is a way of acknowledging that the realm's values, basis for law and foundations for political and social life depend on biblical tradition as it has been mediated to the nation by the church. Fundamental beliefs, such as the dignity and freedom of the individual person, the importance of the family for society, the obligation of service to the community and to the disadvantaged within it, are deeply rooted in the biblical witness in general and in the person and teaching of Jesus Christ in particular.

The Christian gospel is by nature non-coercive (even though the church has not always been) and the great achievement of the Enlightenment was to liberate the Christlike virtue of tolerance from the clutches of unscrupulous politicians and churchmen. At the same time, however, in its refusal to privilege any religious tradition, the Enlightenment cut off values such as human dignity, freedom and tolerance from their roots in the Judaeo-Christian tradition. One of the tasks of social and political reconstruction is to enable society to see the connection between its basic values and the belief system from which they spring and without which they may be difficult to justify. Inalienable human dignity, for instance, makes sense if we believe that all human beings have been made in the image of God and that God has a purpose for humanity as a whole and for particular individuals as well. Take away the belief, and we are left with a free-standing value that can be challenged and even rejected in the cause of ethnic chauvinism or mere commercial self-interest.

When the monarch pledges to uphold the Christian faith,

this is an acknowledgement of the very basis on which the institutions, beliefs and values of the nation depend. The Christian faith is distinctive in many respects and people of other faiths will not always be able to affirm its distinctiveness. For example, one of the leading features of the coronation is to declare the monarch's dependence on divine providence. Naturally, the representatives of non-theistic religions, such as certain kinds of Buddhism, will not be able to affirm what is a basic Christian belief. Other religious traditions that do not see a distinction between what is Caesar's and what is God's may not be able to understand Christianity's (long overdue) renunciation of coercive power on which tolerance of dissent is based.

It may be that, in the future, the monarch and the nation do not wish to affirm the Christian basis of national polity. If that happens then another basis will have to be sought. I suspect, however, that such is not the case and is unlikely to be in the foreseeable future. Any planning for a future coronation, therefore, should proceed on the assumption that the nation wants to reaffirm the Christian basis of national life from which its leading values derive.

One of these values is tolerance of other ways of viewing the world and human destiny, and of allowing these alternative worldviews to contribute to national life without jeopardising the fundamentals on which this life is based. This is why the church should be at once clear about the Christian basis of society *and* welcoming of those of other faiths and of none.

In terms of the coronation, this will mean that representatives of faith communities have an honoured place and are able to bring their greetings and good wishes to the monarch.

It cannot mean, as some have suggested, that they should have places *in the sanctuary*. For one thing, I doubt whether the representatives of some faiths, Jews and Muslims for example, would want to be in a Christian sanctuary. The church should also take care, moreover, that at this, as at any service, nothing is done contrary to or indicative of any departure from the doctrine of the Church of England.

The coronation is not merely a civic or national event in which the church is simply being asked to inaugurate a reign. It is a fundamentally Christian ceremony and its setting within a service of Holy Communion is to indicate its character. The monarch communicates to demonstrate that the church's Supreme Governor is truly a communicant in a church where he or she has jurisdiction but also defers to those who have responsibility for ordering the life of the church. Certainly, there are occasions when it is inappropriate to have Holy Communion, but the coronation is not one of them.

We should be preparing, therefore, for a coronation that remains Christian in character and ecumenical in the involvement of other Christian churches. It should be an event where people of other faiths have an honoured place and are invited to contribute in a way consistent with the nature of the service. Such integrity will honour Christ and will evoke genuine respect among our friends of other faiths – and of none.

Dissent in the Anglican tradition

It is often thought that established churches exist only to sustain and justify the existing social and political order.

There is little doubt that this happens, and happens in the Church of England. Much of the church's liturgy can be seen to reflect the social and political order of its time.[11] We have seen how the system of appointments has also been used to reflect particular social and political views in the church's leadership. This much is to be expected. What is perhaps more surprising is that the Church of England also has a strong tradition of dissent. It is true that the so-called dissenters and nonconformists have paid a heavy price in terms of imprisonment, exile and social ostracism, but much of this is also true of those who dared to differ *within the church itself*. The martyrs on both sides of the Reformation divide are perhaps a good point of departure: John Fisher, a predecessor of mine as Bishop of Rochester, went to the scaffold because he refused to go further than agreeing that the king was supreme head of the Church of England in so far as the law of Christ allows and because he refused to admit that Henry VIII's marriage to Catherine of Aragon was null and void and the issue was illegitimate. On the other side, another predecessor of mine, Nicholas Ridley, was burned along with Hugh Latimer by the fanatic Queen Mary. It was Latimer who said those famous words to Ridley: 'Be of good comfort, Master Ridley, and play the man. We shall this day light such a candle, by God's grace in England, as I trust shall never be put out!'[12]

In the next century, too, there were those who suffered on both sides during the Commonwealth and at the time of the Restoration. Another Bishop of Rochester, John Warner, was deprived of his bishopric and was forced into hiding, surviving on the generosity of relatives and friends. At the Restoration, however, the tables were turned: John Warner was able to return to his see and to establish the famous Bromley College in thanksgiving. At the same time, 2,000 clergy who refused to conform to an episcopal and royalist church were deprived of their livings.

Towards the end of the seventeenth century, a large number of bishops, clergy and lay people refused to take the Oath of Allegiance to the newly arrived William and Mary on the grounds that they had already taken such an oath to the exiled James II and his successors. The bishops and clergy were deprived, but the Non-Jurors, as they came to be called, became an important movement that saw the church as a spiritual society with its own distinctive life. They emphasised the importance of liturgical worship and, for an extended period, conducted negotiations for closer unity with the Orthodox. They survived until well into the eighteenth century and provided the connection between the 'High church' Carolines of the seventeenth century and the Oxford Movement of the nineteenth. They were also influential in the revision of the Scottish Episcopal liturgy of 1764, a rite with acknowledged Eastern features, which was taken to America by Samuel Seabury, the first American Episcopalian bishop, who was consecrated in the Scottish Episcopal Church.[13] This liturgy, which is quite distinctive, has been highly influential in the further development of Anglican worship.

The Oxford Movement, which is usually regarded as beginning with John Keble's assize sermon on National Apostasy, preached on 14 July 1833, also emphasised the divine origin of the church. The state certainly had a role in unifying society and in balancing the claims of one section against those of another, but it could not have any *spiritual* authority over the church. The immediate issue was, of course, the suppression of ten Irish bishoprics and the bone of contention was not *whether* they ought to be suppressed but *who* had the right to do it. The church could not allow state interference in matters that had to do with its divine constitution. Some have thought that the real agenda of the Oxford Movement's Tractarians was disestablishment. Certainly many had sympathy with such an aim and, indeed, Tractarian influence in the disestablishment of the churches in Ireland and in Wales cannot be discounted. What is perhaps more remarkable is the amazing influence that the Oxford Movement has had in the development of the Anglican communion outside the British Isles. From South Africa to New Zealand the church began to see itself as an autonomous organisation with responsibility for its own life, as well as a mission to the nation. It has often been remarked that the prophetic stance of the Church of the Province of Southern Africa during the years of apartheid would not have been possible without its Tractarian formation. There were, of course, many different emphases among Catholic Anglicans, but, because of their belief in the distinctiveness of the church as the bearer of divine revelation, they were bound to allow a more prophetic role to the church and its leaders.[14]

Can an established church be prophetic?

In recent years, establishment has not prevented the Church of England as a whole, and various leaders within it, from exercising a prophetic role. In fact, it is possible to claim that establishment has sometimes provided the opportunity and the means for speaking forthrightly. If Bishop George Bell's condemnation of indiscriminate Allied bombing of German cities can be compared with Robert Runcie's Falklands sermon, in which he asked for prayers for families of the dead on both sides of the war, then William Temple's contribution on post-war regeneration can be said to be an antecedent of *Faith in the City*, the report on the state of the inner cities and the outer estates in the 1980s. During this period, the church often acted as the only effective opposition to a very confident government with a clear agenda and an ideology to go with it.[15] The focus is, however, shifting slowly from the social and political arena, to the frontiers of personal and social morality (much more closely connected than old-style liberalism will allow). Questions about the nature and purpose of marriage and the family, respect for the human person, especially at the beginning and the end of life, and the possibilities of 'made to order' human beings need to be addressed with greater clarity as there are many looking to the church for guidance in these areas.[16]

A church in exile?

The Wakeham Commission on the reform of the House of Lords recognises the role of religion in society and, particularly, of the Church of England. In its proposals it seeks to provide places for the representation of other churches and other faith communities, while retaining a significant place for the Church of England. The basis for its recommendations, however, is not that the church is steward of the tradition that has been influential in the formation of the nation's institutions but that it represents a significant number of people. The overall goal is to encourage 'moral conversations' among people of different points of view.[17] Obviously this is at variance with those arguments that still give the Judaeo-Christian moral and spiritual framework a fundamental place in national life but that, at the same time, welcome contributions from people of other faiths or of none.

Devolution and the emergence of regional assemblies of various kinds have also tended to recognise the place of religion and, some at least, have provided seats for faith communities. This is greatly to be welcomed but, once again, there is little awareness that Christianity needs to be acknowledged in a special way. Decisions are increasingly likely to be made in terms of public opinion, which, in turn, is more and more distant from its spiritual roots. The spiritual resources of the faith communities in terms of hope, perseverance and commitment need to be called on if they are to be more than 'neutral' brokers and providers of buildings and volunteers.

Some understand this growing marginalisation of the church as an opportunity. Just as there is a time for settlement and for contributing to the emergence of a common framework, so there is a time for accepting the reality of 'exile'. The well-known biblical scholar Walter Brueggemann, from the literature of exile in the Older Testament, brings questions to bear on his own situation in the United States of America. In the light of the biblical metaphor of 'exile' he sees the contemporary American situation as analogous to the exile of the Jewish people in Babylon. American Christians also live in a hostile and alien culture where the basic assumptions and values are contrary to the gospel.[18] Brueggemann's analysis of the church in the context of American society will find a ready echo in many other parts of the Western world: here too claims of neutrality often mask a desire to deny a meaningful say to any religious tradition. There is little recognition of the enormous role played by Christianity in the emergence and development of Western cultures. Indifference to the distinctives of different faiths and belief systems leads to short-term utilitarian decisions in the public arena without regard to basic spiritual insights; for example, regarding inalienable human dignity and considerations of the ultimate common good. It may be that the proper autonomy of faith communities will come under increasing pressure in terms of use of their premises, if they are receiving government grants, for example, or in terms of the employment of staff in their institutions, or even the spiritual services they offer.

However we look at the situation, it is clear that Christianity is no longer 'fashionable'; people do not belong because it is 'the done thing' and the views of Christians, including those of church leaders, are no longer 'privileged' or seen as mediating a wisdom on which society is based. In such a context some have begun to argue that churches should see themselves more and more as *moral communities*. A moral community is one closely integrated that has shared beliefs, not least about morality and behaviour. According to the philosopher Alasdair MacIntyre, such communities are, at first, those to which we belong naturally: the family, the neighbourhood, the tribe. It is from here that our moral journey begins and, as we continue in the search for the good, which must be at the same time individual and communal, we may realise the limitations and even the dysfunction of these natural communities. This does not, however, lessen their importance.[19]

Churches cannot, of course, easily be such natural communities. If they are to be moral communities, this will have to be based on a common understanding that the good can be pursued by acknowledging that, in God's providence, the church is a distinct community with its own distinctive values and a particular way of expressing them in its own life and in relations with the wider world. The church is a light set on a high place (Matthew 5:14–16) and lives in a way that sets an example of justice and peace. It is in the fellowship of local Christian communities that the skills of following Jesus are passed on. These will have to do with creating strong relationships of friendship and of mutual aid.

There will be an emphasis on reconciliation, as well as advocacy of the weak. It should be clear, however, that just as other moral communities can be criticised, so can the church. Such a way of conceiving the church should not then prevent internal or external criticism of policies, whether to do with the church's own life or with its mission to the world beyond.

In an important address to the University of Cambridge, Dr David Hope, the Archbishop of York, looked to a much more communitarian and dynamic model of the church. For him it is the experience of communion with God's very life which creates that fellowship in the church that is fundamentally relational rather than institutional. He reminds us that the future is of a 'diaspora-church', which no longer relies on widespread public support for the fulfilment of its mission. It will be a 'community of communities' built up from below as a result of people freely coming together, rather than being imposed from above.[20]

The church should, then, value its established role for as long as it lasts. While the nation still seeks to hear the church's view on national and local issues, the church should be willing to provide a voice in national and local bodies. Such a place is one of tremendous privilege and should not lightly be thrown away. It gives the church opportunities for sharing its vision of the common good, for contributing to national and civic life and, in these ways, commending the gospel of Jesus Christ. At the same time, however, the church needs to recognise that such a situation may not last for ever. It has to prepare itself for an experience of 'exile', when it does not, automatically, have a seat at the table and when the dominant assumptions of the culture are indifferent or hostile to the gospel values the church seeks to promote. The strengthening of local Christian communities, of professional networks, of Christian institutions, for example in the areas of education, pastoral care and community building, is essential if the church is to continue being salt *and* light in this new millennium.

Church and state in the world of Islam and elsewhere

I am very conscious, of course, that most of our attention has been given to the relations between church and state in the Western context, though Southern Africa and Latin America have not been forgotten. There is, however, the very large and very sensitive world of Islam. Relations between church and the state are not only crucial here but differ widely from country to country, even if common themes are discernible. Are Christians equal citizens in Islamic countries? Do they share in a common franchise with their Muslim neighbours or must they always be separate and elect their own representatives? Does the *Shari'ah*, or Islamic law, apply to them? These questions arise in many Islamic contexts and are addressed by many Christians and Muslims. Here we cannot discuss these matters except to note that they exist.[21]

Issues arising from the rapid growth of the church in countries like China also need to be recognised. Totalitarian regimes, like the one in Burma, are also involved in the persecution of Christians, and Christians, both Burmese and others, have to decide what attitude to take towards such a government. The State Department of the USA now regards Christians as among the most persecuted groups in the world.[22] We can be thankful, indeed, that there are organisations in many parts of the world that are not only studying these issues but are active in relieving need and in lobbying international opinion. Although the remit of this book does not permit detailed discussion of their concerns, we must pray for them and co-operate with them in their work, wherever we can.

And Finally . . .

When people have asked me these last few months what I have been writing about, I have tended to say that in my mind's eye the title of the book has always been *Shapes of the Church to Come*. I hope that the reader has also seen it like that. We were concerned at the beginning to discern how the church is being shaped from *the outside*: what pressures are there on the church in a world where nothing is sacrosanct and where every authority is challenged? How is changing demography in a very mobile world affecting ideas about belonging and believing? We have considered what is *positive* about our age and culture and how the Christian faith can relate to it. A fresh awareness of the innateness of spirituality and of moral responsibility was pinpointed as a significant element in our world today. We have also seen, however, the seriousness of sin, as it is acknowledged in contemporary art and literature, and the Christian account of how God deals with it in Christ's work of reconciliation – a work the church seeks to continue.

The shapes of the church are determined, however, not

only from without but also from *within*: the faith that the church has received and which it seeks to pass on in every age and culture also determines what the church is to be. We considered here the place of the Bible in the church and how it relates to the receiving and the passing on of faith that is going on all the time. We saw how Scripture can be seen as both inspired and inspiring. We asked what it affirmed of our spiritual destiny, what it confirmed in our own experience and what it corrected in a world gone wrong. We were aware that elements of the faith can be neglected or even forgotten and that new situations can bring them to light again so that the church is, indeed, like the householder who brings out of his treasure things both old and new (Matthew 13:52). Not every new situation, however, can be dealt with by simply rediscovering an aspect of the faith that has been neglected. Sometimes the church finds itself in uncharted territory; we have attempted to identify the principles that should govern its life and teaching in such circumstances.

The mystery of the church is so rich and deep that we cannot wholly understand it. That is why we need models, metaphors and images of the church to help us to see its nature and task more clearly. We have looked at the different ways in which the church has been imaged and thought about. We have considered also the strengths and weaknesses of each. The Bible and the unvarying practice of the church do, however, provide us with some essential ways of being 'church' that are good for every age and every place. Beyond these, though, a great deal of experiment and innovation is possible and we have examined some new ways of being 'church'. We have looked at the different ways in which the importance of *small Christian communities* is being emphasised and also at the ways in which larger congregations can be given a more *missionary* orientation. We have considered the different ways in which churches are *planted* or *grown* and the differences between the two approaches. We have seen that it is important to be aware of the *assumptions* that underlie missionary approaches and to examine them in the light of the Bible and the church's history.

Given that the church is being shaped in these different ways, what kind of ministry does it require? Once again, we have tried to relate the resources of the Bible and of Tradition to our needs today. We have welcomed the increasing realisation that each of the baptised has a ministry and also the varieties of authorised and ordained ministries possible today. In particular, we have looked at the ministry of women and the church and how ministers should be remunerated, rewarded and affirmed in today's church.

We have been conscious throughout that the body of Christ is divided and one of our aims has been to build up the unity of all those who call themselves Christian. We have considered the different impulses towards unity and how these have been promoted or impeded. We have looked at the importance of the local in the building up of Christian unity and noted some fresh emphases in this area. What kind of unity are we seeking and is it enough? We have seen how the ecumenical movement has changed churches and families of churches and that this process is a continuing one. We have also noted the tension between the wider agenda of promoting the unity of all humankind, even of the created universe (Ephesians 1:10), and the more specific aim of promoting the unity of the church. We have seen, nevertheless, that our Lord's High Priestly prayer brings the two together because the unity of believers is necessary for the world to believe (John 17:21).

Finally, we have considered how a changing culture is bringing about a new situation in terms of relations between church and state. Once again, we have asked what resources were provided by the Bible and the history of the church and have sought to understand them in the light of our own context. We have looked at both the value of having a formal link with the state and the *limitations* this might impose on the church. The changes we are seeing all around us may lead to a situation where the church is no longer at the *centre* but has to find its strength on the *margins*. We must be equipped for such an eventuality, even while we continue to take the opportunities still available to us.

The Bible and the history of the church provide us with exciting models, images and metaphors for the church. The worldwide church has much to teach us about 'shapes' of the church today. It is the task of each local Christian community, of denominational leaders and of national church bodies to ask what can be appropriated from the Bible, from the historic resources of the church and from current practice elsewhere for the sake of mission in particular places and social contexts. Having considered our fast-changing world and a changing church within it, we can bring our thinking together to an end by reflecting on what is said about Christians in the early *Epistle to Diognetus*:

> The distinction between Christians and others, is neither in country nor language nor customs. They do not dwell in their own cities, nor do they speak a strange tongue nor have a different kind of life. They do not claim to be intellectually superior.

> While living in cities of different civilizations, they follow local custom in clothing, food and other matters, yet they also show forth their other citizenship. They dwell in their native land, but as if they are strangers. They share all things as citizens, and suffer all things as strangers. Every foreign country is home to them, and every homeland is a foreign country. Like everyone else, they marry and have children, but they do not destroy their offspring. They are hospitable but they are also pure. Although they are 'in the flesh', they do not live 'according to the flesh'. They are on earth, but their citizenship is in heaven. Not only do they obey existing laws, they surpass them in their own lives. They love everyone and yet are persecuted. They are unknown and yet they are condemned. They are put to death but are alive, nevertheless. They are poor but make many rich; they lack all things and have all things in abundance. Although abused, they bless, when insulted they render honour. Even if they do good, they are treated as evil-doers. When they suffer, they rejoice as those who have life. (5:1–16)[1]

However we respond to our situation and whatever shapes the church assumes, we shall be effective in our witness and service if we live by this vision.

A Study Guide for Groups

Introduction

The year 1901 was a notable one. It was the year in which Queen Victoria died and the twentieth century began. In many ways the Church of England then was very different from the one we know today. The ministry of lay people, for example, was far more restricted. (Those licensed as Readers – an office revived in 1866 – were not allowed to administer the chalice until 1941!) The position of women in the church was scarcely debated – in fact, women did not yet have the right to vote. The start of broadcasting as we know it was still some twenty years in the future, and there were few competitors to church on Sundays. Towns and cities were growing and the need for new churches continued apace.

On a lighter note, parish clergy communicated most often by handwritten letter and by meeting people face to face. The almost universal telephone and email had still to arrive on the scene. Transport was either on foot or by horsepower!

It would be some decades before private cars would be seen regularly on parsonage drives.

Many of the present challenges facing the Church of England and the other churches, however, would have been surprisingly familiar to our predecessors. *The Condition of England*, published in 1909, praises the churches for their active endeavour in seeking to influence the lives of people, and notes widespread appreciation for their humanitarian and social efforts.[1] It also adds that their 'definite dogmatic teaching seems to count for little at all. They labour steadily on amid a huge indifference.'

Five years earlier, correspondence in the *Daily Telegraph* under the title 'Do We Believe?' had shown much scepticism among that paper's middle-class readers.[2] Secularism was gaining strength, and both laity and clergy were beginning to question publicly the virgin birth, the miracles and physical resurrection of Jesus, and the historical basis of Christianity.[3]

The Great War of 1914–18 gave rise to much heart-searching, and to an appraisal of the Church of England's mission. In 1919 five 'Committees of Inquiry', appointed by the Archbishops of Canterbury and York – into the church's teaching office, its worship, evangelism, administration and involvement in industry – produced five reports, all acknowledging the Church of England's failure. The delivery of its message was 'out of touch with the thoughts and ideas of the time'. Its clergy needed better training. It was out of touch with ordinary people. The Prayer Book needed urgent reform. The laity needed to be involved more in worship and taught how to pray in private.[4]

At the start of the twenty-first century, with all that has

happened both in society and in the churches, this book has addressed many of those selfsame questions. It has encouraged us to look forward – to the next hundred years – rather than back. And that is important. Should we be disheartened that so little has changed? One response is to say that we should not be, but that we should rise to the challenges of our own time. It is up to each generation to find its own appropriate responses, and that is what this book seeks to do.

In our groups, congregations and parishes, paying heed to what Richard Hooker, the Anglican divine, called the three-legged stool of Scripture, Tradition (with both a capital and a lower case 't') and Reason, it is important to consider our calling, both as individuals and as a local church. Hooker said that the church is not a static but an organic institution, and that things will change from time to time. That encourages us to identify and engage with the issues likely to face the church in this coming century and to consider how we address them. This book encourages us, too, to confront the challenges and opportunities facing us here and now, and to ask how, in the light of our understanding, we may best respond in our own context.

Each of this book's chapters could stimulate discussion and debate. This Study Guide is offered as a help to structure that discussion and debate within a framework of Bible study and prayer. It is intended for use with home and other groups over eight sessions, which may be weekly, or less frequent. (Individual readers may also find it helpful.) I trust that use of the Study Guide will lead, ultimately, to a deeper understanding, to action, and to the effective proclamation of the word and work of God through his people and church in the coming years.

Preparation

It will help if the leader is someone who can encourage the contributions of all members of the group. She or he will also need to spend some time in preparation, reading through the appropriate chapter, and perhaps thinking of music, songs, poems, pictures and prayers that will add to the group's understanding and enjoyment. The group members will need to bring Bibles with them (remember to have spares for any who forget). It is also a good idea to have notebooks and pens available. Comfortable chairs and a welcoming atmosphere always help a group give of its best, and the materials are designed to work best with groups of up to twelve people.

Timing

Each session could last up to an hour and a half, though detailed timings for each section are not suggested – it depends on the group. Some groups may want to spend longer on some sections than others. I have not envisaged that all groups will find time to tackle all the suggested questions and have taken this into account.

What is included?

There are a number of parts to each session. The first section, 'Aim', introduces the topic for the session. The next section, 'Getting started', presents questions designed to stimulate conversation and discussion. The 'Bible reading' and 'Reflection' sections follow, focusing on a particular aspect of the topic being discussed, encouraging members of the group to relate their experiences and comments to Scripture. 'Moving on' is the time when members of the group really get to grips with the subject of the session and, if appropriate, decide on what practical responses they can make. The session ends with a time of 'Prayer'. There is a suggested prayer printed but some groups may want to include open prayer, and may also want to allow time for singing.

Session 1: Is There a Gospel for the Twenty-first Century?

Aim

To explore ways in which the 'good news' can be communicated effectively in our own age, and to consider the different needs of different groups of people.

Getting started

- Start by asking members of the group to introduce themselves and to share, briefly, how they heard the 'good news' and how they responded to it.
- Encourage the group to talk about the different kinds of people who make up the area in which they live. Zoë, our example, is a single mother, running a home and family, and with a demanding job outside the home. Time is at a premium for her. What other sorts of people live in the neighbourhood?
- Do members of the group agree that 'spirituality' is deeply wired into everyone, as this chapter suggests? What examples can they offer to support their view?

- You may want to ask members of the group which aspects of Chapter 1 they found most interesting and which most challenging. Make a note of the points they raise for later.

Bible reading

Read John 1:1–18 – the prologue to John's Gospel.

Reflection

- In speaking of 'the Word' (*logos*), the prologue to John's Gospel connects both with Greek thought (which understood the 'Word' as the rational principle that governs all things) and with Jewish thought (which uses it as a way of referring to God). How does this help us understand that the gospel of Jesus Christ is 'for every age and clime'?
- Spend some time thinking about the 'big story' that this passage encapsulates. What does it tell us of God and his purposes?
- The prologue talks of those who believe as 'children of God'. What do members of the group think that means?
- How does the passage help us understand the meaning of repentance and reconciliation?

Moving on

- What, in our own society, can the gospel not tolerate, what can it tolerate for the time being, and what should it endorse and transform?
- How do members of the group react to Bishop Richard Holloway's claim that 'it is possible to make moral

judgments, to engage in moral dialogue about the common good and about our own flourishing without an explicit appeal to revelation'?

- What are some possible reasons for the churches 'soft-pedalling' traditional teaching in the area of evil?
- Why is the gospel's capacity to heal people and relationships important in the church's mission today?
- What does the group make of Dr Grace Davie's idea of 'believing without belonging' – that people may be Christians without belonging to any church? What does the gospel have to say to them? And what of those who 'belong without believing'? How can they best be encouraged in their faith?
- What aspects of the gospel would members of the group want to emphasise in sharing the good news with the different kinds of people they identified in 'Getting started'?
- Have the points of interest, or the challenges, identified in 'Getting started' been picked up and sufficiently discussed?

> 'Spirituality has become an all-purpose description of what people feel to be missing from their lives rather than of what they hope to discover' . . . This spiritual search is, 'A symptom of collective uncertainty in an age when the traditional institutions of church, family and community appear to be breaking down.'[5]

Prayer

May we know the power of the Father,
the saving love of the Son,
and the guidance of the Holy Spirit,

as we seek the wisdom to meet others in their need
and to lead them to you, our God.
Help us to bring light where there is darkness,
faith where there is doubt,
hope where there is fear,
and love where there is hatred.
Take the ways and thoughts of this age,
correct what is wrong,
and convert them to your loving purpose,
through Jesus Christ, our Lord. Amen.

Session 2: Is There a Future for the Church?

Aim

To explore ways in which the church is shaped by pressures from both the outside and the inside, and to use these deliberations as a springboard for considering new ways of being church.

Getting started

- Start this session by considering the situation of your own church building. Why, when and how did it come into being? Whether it is ancient or modern, what was the vision for it?
- How important is the past as we look to the future? Should the church be open to change?
- What part does the Bible play in the life of your church and in your own life? How relevant is it to life in the twenty-first century?
- You may want to ask members of the group which aspects of Chapter 2 they found most interesting and which most challenging. Make a note of the points they raise for later.

Bible reading

Read 2 Timothy 3:14–17.

Reflection

- What does it mean when verse 16 says that all Scripture is 'God-breathed'? (Bear in mind that when this letter was written, the Scripture was our Older Testament and perhaps a few of the early apostolic documents.)
- The author writes that Timothy should continue in what he has learned and has become convinced of, 'because you know those from whom you learned it, and how from infancy you have known the holy Scriptures . . .'. Why does he attach such importance to one generation passing on the faith to the next, and why is it important that Timothy knew the Scriptures from infancy? Are these issues important today for the future of the church? If so, why?
- The passage speaks of Scripture as useful for teaching, rebuking, correcting and training in righteousness. How true is that today?
- In the light of this passage, do you think Christians should believe the Bible is the word of God and relevant to every age, or should it be seen as a piece of ancient literature? Or is there another answer?

Moving on

- How much attention should the church pay to outside pressures and the shape of the world around it?

- What do you understand by Tradition?
- In what ways has the Bible inspired the way you live your life, your attitudes and principles?
- God as Creator and God as Redeemer are two important examples of what Scripture affirms. How do you think Christianity would manage without either?
- How important is what Scripture has to say about issues such as family and community relationships in today's world, both in what it confirms and what it corrects?
- How far can or should the church go in 're-receiving' Scripture on issues such as slavery, the position of the poor, and attitudes to women?
- What sort of a future might the church have if Scripture were to be ignored?
- Have the points of interest, or the challenges, identified in 'Getting started' been picked up and sufficiently discussed?

I read my Bible to know what people ought to do and my newspaper to know what they are doing. (J H Newman, 1801–90)

Prayer

Most gracious Father, we most humbly beseech thee for thy holy catholic church. Fill it with all truth; in all truth with thy peace. Where it is corrupt, purge it; where it is in error, direct it; where anything is remiss, reform it; where it is right, strengthen and confirm it; where it is in want, furnish it; where it is divided, heal it, and unite it in thy love; through Jesus Christ our Lord. Amen. (Archbishop William Laud, 1573–1645)

Session 3: Fundamentals of Being Church

Aim

To consider the 'shapes' of the church, from house churches to a worldwide movement, and to begin to think about how those 'shapes' may be relevant for the twenty-first century.

Getting started

- In the group, start by thinking of the group itself, probably meeting in a home. What do people think of the experience? Identify some of the advantages and disadvantages. What if this was the only place for the church to meet week by week?
- How meaningful and relevant is it for members of the group to think of themselves as members of a universal or worldwide church?
- Why should a home church or local church need to be part of a bigger organisation?
- You may want to ask members of the group which aspects

of Chapter 3 they found most interesting and which most challenging. Make a note of the points they raise for later.

Bible reading

Read Matthew 28:16–20 and Colossians 4:10–16.

Reflection

- At the end of Matthew's Gospel, Jesus' commission to the disciples is to 'make disciples of all nations'. What do you understand by this?
- Where might the disciples and the new followers have met, and what might have happened at their meetings?
- How important do you think it was for the early church to be well organised? What does the passage from Colossians say about that organisation?
- Consider Paul's role in the early church. Share briefly some of the reasons why it might be considered an important one.

Moving on

- Homes were important places for teaching, crucial (alongside missionaries and catechists) for spreading the good news throughout the ancient world. Why should that have been the case?
- When Christians from one area came together to meet in one place, it was usual for them to celebrate the Eucharist there rather than in their own home. What significance might this have had?

- One of the main hallmarks of churches as they grew from being isolated entities was their interdependence and interrelatedness, caring for one another's spiritual and material needs. How much do you think this characterises the church today? And how much does it characterise your church?
- One meaning of the term 'catholic' is 'universal', and the universal church is 'represented' in the local churches, as well as being 'made up' of the local churches. In what ways does your church show that it is part of the universal church?
- If your church is Anglican, what does it mean to be a part of the Anglican communion? (If your church is not Anglican, what does it mean to be a part of whatever international body represents your church?)
- What do you think today's 'big issues' are that the church needs to speak out on with one worldwide voice?
- Have the points of interest, or the challenges, identified in 'Getting started' been picked up and sufficiently discussed?

There is no one else who is seriously bidding for the heart of the world except Jesus. There is no one else on the field. (Anonymous)

Prayer

Most gracious Father, grant to your church
strength, wisdom and discernment
through your Holy Spirit.
Keep it faithful to the truth of the gospel,

and sustain it with faith in the power of Christ.
Grant wisdom and fellowship to all our leaders,
that they may bring release to those
who are under the power of sin.
May we, your people, be a living witness to the whole
world;
make each one a minister of the word,
bringing the blessing of peace to many,
through Jesus Christ, our Lord. Amen.

Session 4: Models of the Church

Aim

To explore biblical 'models' of the church, and to discuss their relevance for the church of the twenty-first century.

Getting started

- Which 'model' of the church most nearly matches the church or churches to which members of the group belong?
- Why is it important and useful to understand something about these 'models'?
- What do members of the group understand when the church is talked of as a 'mystery', in the theological sense?
- You may want to ask members of the group which aspects of Chapter 4 they found most interesting and which most challenging. Make a note of the points they raise for later.

Bible reading

Read 1 Peter 2:4–10.

Reflection

- This description of the church as a building made up of 'living stones', with Jesus as the cornerstone or capstone, recalls the image found in Ephesians 2:20. (The church in central Milton Keynes today has 'Christ the Cornerstone' as its dedication.) Discuss what this image or metaphor means to members of the group.
- The image is reinforced by quotations from the Older Testament's book of Isaiah and the book of Psalms. Why does the group think the writer of the letter did this?
- What does the group think the 'spiritual sacrifices' are that Christians are called to offer (v. 5)? (It may help to look at Romans 12:1; Philippians 4:18; Hebrews 13:15–16.)
- In verse 9, what impact do you imagine the different descriptions of early Christians had on those who first read or heard the letter? What is their impact now?

Moving on

- Thinking of the church as the 'body of Christ', does the group believe that this is the best 'model' of the church? If so, why? If not, why not?
- Discuss the appeal of some of the other 'models' mentioned in this chapter. Which ones seem to fit the group's

own image(s) of the church most closely, and which fit least well?

- How helpful is it that the 'models' overlap and are not mutually exclusive?
- All the 'models' mentioned focus on the church as people and not on the church as buildings. Where is the focus of today's church, in the experience of the group – on people or buildings? What does that focus say about the church to the world outside?
- If the group had to come up with a new 'model' or metaphor for the church, what might it be? (It may be interesting to ask members of the group to think of an animal that they think most closely resembles the church they know. Ask them to say why they chose the animal they did.)
- Have the points of interest, or the challenges, identified in 'Getting started' been picked up and sufficiently discussed?

The Church is a family. To be Church, to live as a church, means to live as a family, aware that we need others. (Leonard Doohan)

Prayer

You, Lord, are with your family;
your presence fills us;
your presence is love.

You, Lord, are with your family;
your presence fills us;
your presence is peace.

You, Lord, are with your family;
your presence fills us;
your presence is light.

You, Lord, are with your family;
your presence fills us;
your presence is all.

Amen.

Session 5: Ways of Being Church

Aim

To explore the different ways in which churches are organised and to discover how different ways of being church are appropriate in different situations.

Getting started

- Ask members of the group to think of the kind of church organisation that best suits them. If they say it's the one they're in at the moment, ask them why that is.
- How much thought have members of the group given to the many different ways of being church? How surprised were they by the variety that exists?
- What message(s) does the group think their church building(s) (or the building where they meet) communicates to outsiders about the faith of the church? What message do they think they should give? (The same could be asked of the church 'fellowship'.)
- You may want to ask members of the group which

aspects of Chapter 5 they found most interesting and which most challenging. Make a note of the points they raise for later.

Bible reading

Read Matthew 25:34–46.

Reflection

- This passage focuses on the importance of serving others. What impact do you think these words might have had on those who first heard them?
- How important should this kind of service be in today's church?
- In her book *Beyond the Good Samaritan* Ann Morisy says that if Christians engage in social action, there must be added value to it. How does this passage help as a reminder of that?
- How might this passage encourage us to understand the place of service to others in our Christian witness?

Moving on

- Why does the group think new ways of 'being church' come about?
- Why is it important to consider a range of ways of 'being church' when planning new work and activities?
- How important in the life of a community is a church building that 'looks like' a church?
- What role should other parts of the community (e.g.

medical and social services, local authorities and education services) play in influencing ways of 'being church'?

- 'Niche' marketing, trying to offer specialised services to identifiable groups of people, is an important contemporary marketing concept. How important is it that the church should try to cater for different 'tastes' and to meet a variety of needs in different ways, both in church services and other ways? Or should people find ways of adapting to what the church offers?
- Which ways of 'being church' does the group think have outlived their usefulness and should be ended?
- How should new ways of 'being church' be monitored, if at all?
- Have the points of interest, or the challenges, identified in 'Getting started' been picked up and sufficiently discussed?

The Russian novelist and social reformer, Leo Tolstoy, tells the story of a man who stopped to give alms to a beggar. To his dismay, he found he had left his money at home. 'I'm sorry, brother, but I have nothing.' 'Never mind, brother,' was the beggar's answer, 'that too was a gift.' The one word 'brother' meant more to him than money.

Prayer

Heavenly Father, bless the church in all its many ways of being, called to serve you as the gathered people of your eternal purpose; keep it steadfast in faith, ready to bear the cost of discipleship, a worthy temple for your presence and filled with a knowledge of your glory.

May we honour one another in love and live as reconcilers and messengers of your peace, ready to serve and eager to do your will, through Jesus Christ, our Lord. Amen.

Session 6: What Kind of Ministry Does the Church Require?

Aim

To explore the kinds of ministry the church needs to encourage and develop in order to meet the needs and demands of the twenty-first century.

Getting started

- Encourage members of the group to talk about the communities in which they live. For many this will be a community based less on geography than on networks – of workmates, of people who have the same leisure interests, of church friends, of people who do the same voluntary work, and so on. Such communities have been called 'virtual' communities, and depend heavily upon personal mobility.
- 'Consumer choice' is a powerful force in the commercial world. Good marketing is vital. How far do group members think the church should go in attempting to respond to the demands of 'consumer choice'?

- What points of contact between the church and its local community can group members identify?
- This session will be concerned with the church's ministry. What different kinds of ministry can members of the group identify in their own church(es)?
- You may want to ask members of the group which aspects of Chapter 6 they found most interesting and which most challenging. Make a note of the points they raise for later.

Bible reading

Read Romans 12:1–8.

Reflection

- What do verses 1–4 have to say about the 'mindset' or attitude of a Christian person? How realistic are they?
- It is one thing 'not to think of yourself more highly than you ought', but how can fellow Christians be encouraged to appreciate and use the gifts they have though are perhaps too modest to acknowledge?
- How are the gifts Paul identifies in verses 6–8 exercised in the church today? What emphasis should be given to each?
- Encourage members of the group to search out some other spiritual gifts mentioned in the Bible. (A good starting point is 1 Corinthians 12!)

Moving on

- Chapter 6 suggests that the church for the twenty-first century will need to be outward-looking and missionary-minded. If that strategy is to work, it will need to be supported by the 'ministry of all the baptised'. What do members of the group understand by that last expression?

- How does the group think that callings to the lay or ordained ministry can best be discerned and tested? What should the role of the local and the wider church be?
- Where does the stipendiary ministry of the clergy fit into the 'grand plan' in the group's view? Is it the best use of resources to continue to fit stipendiary clergy into a 'local' slot, or should some wider role be encouraged?
- What would the impact of the group's view be on non-stipendiary clergy, on lay ministers, such as Readers, Pastoral Assistants and Evangelists, and on others exercising a ministry in a local church?
- What does the group make of John Drane's view that without the missionary dimension, professional pastors will simply preside over institutional decline, doing a reasonably good job but with a dying church as the end result?
- What kind of ministry in the church, in the group's view is appropriate for women?
- Have the points of interest, or the challenges, identified in 'Getting started' been picked up and sufficiently discussed?

'My friends,' said the churchwarden, 'our dear Vicar, as you know, will shortly be leaving us, and I therefore propose we take up a collection to give him a little momentum.'

Prayer

Let me remember my Lord's eagerness,
not to be ministered unto, but to minister;
his sympathy with suffering of every kind;
his meekness of bearing, so that, when reviled
he reviled not again;
his steadiness of purpose in keeping to his appointed task;
his simplicity;
his self-discipline;
his serenity of spirit;
and his complete reliance upon his Father in heaven.

And in each of these ways give me grace to follow in
his footsteps. Amen.

(John Baillie, 1886–1960)

Session 7: One So That the World May Believe

Aim

To discuss ways in which unity among the Christian churches needs to be encouraged locally, nationally and internationally in the twenty-first century.

Getting started

- What experience do members of the group have of local churches working together? How positive have those experiences been?
- How would people outside the local church know that there was more sharing and co-operation between churches? What evidence should there be?
- Encourage the group to share any other examples they know of churches working together effectively.
- You may want to ask members of the group which aspects of Chapter 7 they found most interesting and which most challenging. Make a note of the points they raise for later.

Bible reading

Read John 17:6–21.

Reflection

- Verse 8 speaks of three characteristics of the disciples. What are they and, in the view of the group, are they a sufficient basis for the unity of the church? If not, what else is needed?
- In verse 11, the Greek has the sense of 'that they may *continue* to be one' rather than 'that they may *become* one'. How does the group react to the idea that unity is already given and is not something to be achieved?
- Jesus talks of the same unity existing between the Father and his disciples as exists between the Father and the Son. How, in their understanding, would members of the group describe that unity between the Father and Jesus?
- Unity is not without a purpose. Verse 21 makes that clear. What is the purpose and what would its impact have been on those who first heard those words as John's Gospel has recorded them? What is their impact on the group?

Moving on

- What results do members of the group think the impact of worldwide initiatives in unity have yielded? What do they see as the advantages and disadvantages of the international ecumenical movement?
- The impetus for many ecumenical initiatives in the UK has come because of insistence from below rather than

pressure from above. How does the group feel that national and international church organisations should react in these circumstances?

- How far should the 'distinctives' of each tradition be maintained in, for example, a Local Ecumenical Partnership, if there is a risk that anything else results in 'lowest common denominator' worship and rootless Christian communities?
- In what measure is a 'unity in the Spirit' an acceptable substitute for 'visible unity'?
- How possible is it for the church to be both 'united' and 'diverse'?
- What impact have the workings and affairs of the Anglican communion had on the Church of England, in the view of the group?
- If the fellowship of the church has to be for the sake of the gospel and not the internal relations of the church, how do members of the group feel that advances can be made?
- Have the points of interest, or the challenges, identified in 'Getting started' been picked up and sufficiently discussed?

In a divided Christianity, instead of reading the Bible to assure ourselves that we are right, we would do better to read it to discover where we have not been listening. (Raymond E Brown)

Prayer

O Lord Jesus Christ, who didst pray for thy disciples that they might be one, even as thou art one with the Father: Draw us to thyself, that in common love and obedience to thee we may be united to one another, in the fellowship of the one Spirit, that the world may believe that thou art Lord, to the glory of God the Father. Amen. (Archbishop William Temple)

Session 8: Rendering to Caesar

Aim

To explore the biblical and historical links between church and state, and to discuss the advantages and disadvantages of the Church of England continuing as the established church in England in the twenty-first century.

Getting started

- In the view of the group, what impact does the Church of England as the established church in England have on the local church?
- In a multicultural and multifaith country, where attitudes and values are changing rapidly, what reasons are there for maintaining an established church – a church recognised by the state as having a special position?
- You may want to ask members of the group which aspects of Chapter 8 they found most interesting and which most challenging. Make a note of the points they raise for later.

Bible reading

Read Romans 13:1–7.

Reflection

- Chapters 12 to 15 of the letter to the Romans focus on how to live life as a Christian. Chapter 13 concentrates on the Christian's relationship with the state and with the 'world'. What sort of view does Paul take of the authority of the state?
- Look at Acts 4:19 and 5:29. Paul's attitude in Romans 13:3 seems to be very different. Can (or should) the two views be reconciled? If so, how? If not, why not?
- Turn now to Matthew 22:15–22. How would you describe Jesus' attitude to the state?
- In the Older Testament, find 2 Samuel 12:1–15. Here there is an example of the relationship between the prophets and the monarchy. The prophets, like Nathan, can be seen as a steadying influence, preventing the monarchy (the state) from becoming absolute. How important was that role of the prophets?

Moving on

- How relevant are the examples from the Older Testament in considering the role of the established church today? Is there, for example, a prophetic role for the church that could not be exercised if it were not established?
- What does the group think are the most important features of the 'kingdom of God'?

- Chapter 8 outlines the history of the established church in this country. How relevant is the established church to today's society?
- As far as the church is concerned, what might some of the benefits of establishment, and some of the disadvantages, be?
- How important is it, in the group's view, for representatives of the churches and of other faiths to sit in a reformed House of Lords?
- If the alternative to an established church is a church 'in exile', what might the advantages and disadvantages be?
- Have the points of interest, or the challenges, identified in 'Getting started' been picked up and sufficiently discussed?

A Christian is the most free lord of all, and subject to none; a Christian is the most dutiful servant of all, and subject to everyone. (Martin Luther)

Prayer

Almighty God, by whom alone monarchs reign and princes decree justice, and from whom alone cometh counsel and understanding: We humbly beseech thee to grant thy heavenly wisdom to those who have been called to serve in the parliament of this nation. Grant that, having thy fear always before their eyes, they may lay aside all private interests and partial affections, and take counsel together for the glory of thy name, the maintenance of true religion and justice, and the welfare, peace and unity of the realm; through Jesus Christ our Lord. Amen. (An adaptation of the Prayer for Parliament)

Notes

Chapter 1

1. See further my *Mission and Dialogue: Proclaiming the Gospel Afresh in Every Age* (London: SPCK, 1995), pp 13ff, and also Richard A Batey, *Jesus and the Forgotten City* (Grand Rapids: Baker Book House, 1991).
2. See, for example, John Stambaugh and David Balch, *The Social World of the First Christians* (London: SPCK, 1994).
3. See further Lamin Sanneh, *Translating the Message – The Missionary Impact on Culture* (New York: Orbis, 1989), and my *Citizens and Exiles: Christian Faith in a Plural World* (London: SPCK, 1998), pp 21f.
4. In Vinay Samuel and Christopher Sugden (eds), *Proclaiming Christ in Christ's Way* (Oxford: Regnum, 1989), pp 101ff.
5. *Origins*, CNS Documentary Service, 30th March 1995, pp 679ff.
6. Henry Hill (ed), *Light from the East: A Symposium on*

the Oriental Orthodox and Assyrian Churches (Toronto: Anglican Book Centre, 1988), pp 14ff, 62ff. See also Calvin E Shenk, 'The Ethiopian Orthodox Church's Understanding of Mission', *Mission Studies*, vol 4, No 1 (1987), pp 4ff.

7. Anton Wessels, *Europe: Was It Ever Really Christian*? (London: SCM, 1994).
8. See further Jaroslav Pelikan, *The Excellent Empire: The Fall of Rome and the Triumph of the Church* (San Francisco: Harper and Row, 1987), and William Young, *Patriarch, Shah and Caliph* (Rawalpindi: Christian Study Centre, 1974).
9 See Lesslie Newbigin, *Foolishness to the Greeks* (London: SPCK, 1986), pp 14, 50.
10. See further the Church of England Report *The Search for Faith and the Witness of the Church* (London: CHP, 1996), especially ch 3, and Paul Zahl, *The Protestant Face of Anglicanism* (Grand Rapids: Eerdmans, 1998), ch 5.
11. See the excellent discussion in David Brown's *Tradition and Imagination: Revelation and Change* (Oxford: OUP, 1999), pp 32ff.
12. See further James Beckford and Sophie Gilliat, *The Church of England and Other Faiths in a Multi-Faith Society* (Coventry: University of Warwick, 1996).
13. Grace Davie, *Religion in Britain since 1945: Believing without Belonging* (Oxford: Blackwell, 1994), Robin Gill, *The Myth of the Empty Church* (London: SPCK, 1993), and Church of England Report, *The Search for Faith*, pp 4ff.
14. David Hay and Kate Hunt, *Understanding the Spirituality of People Who Don't Go to Church* (Centre for the Study of

Human Relations, University of Nottingham final report, August 2000).

15. David Hay and Rebecca Nye, *The Spirit of the Child* (London: HarperCollins, 1998). See also Robert Coles, *The Spiritual Life of Children* (Boston: Mifflin, 1990).
16. O'Donovan, *Resurrection and the Moral Order* (Leicester: IVP, 1986), p 190.
17. Internet (http://www.cin.org/jp2ency/versplen.html).
18. Richard Holloway, *Godless Morality* (Canongate, 1991).
19. See further Charles Moule, *The Epistles to the Colossians and to Philemon* (Cambridge: CUP, 1957), pp 123–4.
20. For an outline of such a doctrine of God see my *Citizens and Exiles*, pp 14ff.
21. *The Independent*, 21st June 1993.
22. See further Church of England Report, *The Search for Faith*, pp 150ff.
23. See Russell Stannard, *Science and the Renewal of Belief* (London: SCM, 1982).
24. M Luther, *The Bondage of the Will* (Michigan: Fleming H Revell, 1957, reprinted 1990).
25. Ephesians 20:2.
26. Quoted by James Whyte in *A Dictionary of Pastoral Care* (London: SPCK, 1990), p 193.
27. O Sacks, *The Man Who Mistook His Wife for a Hat* (London: Picador, 1986), p 36, and Church of England Report, *The Search for Faith*, p 18.
28. See further E A Judge's Tyndale lecture 'Cultural Conformity and Innovation in Paul: Some Clues from Contemporary Documents', *Tyndale Bulletin*, vol. 35 (1984), pp 3f, and John Stambaugh and David Balch, *The Social World of the First Christians* (London: SPCK, 1994).

29. See further Moule, *Colossians*, pp 127f.
30. Peter Phan, *Social Thought: Message of the Fathers of the Church* (Wilmington: Michael Glazier, 1984), pp 23f.

Chapter 2

1. See further F F Bruce, *I and II Corinthians* (Grand Rapids: Eerdmans, 1971), pp 137f, Leon Morris, *1 and 2 Thessalonians* (London: Tyndale, 1956), pp 137f, and John Stott, *The Message of Thessalonians* (Leicester: IVP, 1991), pp 177f.
2. Article 25 of the 39 Articles of Religion in *The Book of Common Prayer*.
3. On the formation of the Canon see Charles Moule, *The Birth of the New Testament* (London: A & C Black, 1962), pp 178ff, and James Dunn, *Unity and Diversity in the New Testament* (London: SCM, 1990), pp 369ff.
4. See further J N D Kelly, *The Pastoral Epistles* (London: A & C Black, 1963), pp 197ff.
5. See, for example, I Howard Marshall, *The Gospel of Luke* (Exeter: Paternoster, 1978), pp 72f, and also his commentary on *Acts* (Grand Rapids: Eerdmans, 1980), p 72.
6. M Nazir-Ali, *Jesus Christ in Today's World*, in Gordon Kuhrt (ed), *To Proclaim Afresh* (London: SPCK, 1995). See also David Bebbington, *Evangelicalism in Modern Britain* (London: Unwin Hyman, 1989), pp 12ff and 86ff.
7. Gabriele Finaldi, *The Image of Christ* (London: National Gallery, 2000), and Anthony Green, RA, *Resurrection: A Pictorial Sculpture for the Millennium* (London: Napier Jones, 1999).

8. See also my *Citizens and Exiles*, ch 12.
9. ARCIC, *The Gift of Authority* (Toronto and London: Anglican Book Centre/CTS, 1999), p 19.
10. See further my *Islam: A Christian Perspective* (Exeter: Paternoster, 1983), pp 42f.
11. Gerhard von Rad, *Genesis* (London: SCM, 1972), pp 66f.
12. See further his trilogy *One World, Science and Creation* and *Science and Providence* (London: SPCK, 1986–89).
13. H Montefiore, *The Probability of God* (London: SCM, 1985), and J Lovelock, *Gaia: A New Look at Life on Earth* (Oxford: OUP, 1979). See also Paul Davies, *The Mind of God* (London: Penguin, 1992), and my *Citizens and Exiles*, pp 24ff.
14. Nazir-Ali, *Citizens and Exiles*, ch 9.
15. George Herbert, 'The Sinner' in *The Works of George Herbert* (Ware: Wordsworth Library, 1994), p 30.
16. See further Gustav Aulen, *Christus Victor* (London: SPCK, 1950).
17. Nazir-Ali, *Citizens and Exiles*, ch 4.
18. T S Eliot, 'East Coker IV' in *Four Quartets* (London: Faber, 1970), p 29, Henri Nouwen, *The Wounded Healer* (New York: Doubleday, 1979), Rowan Williams, 'Reflections on René Girard', unpublished paper, and James Alison, *Knowing Jesus* (London: SPCK, 1993).
19. For an account of various Orthodox positions see Aram Keshishian, *Orthodox Perspectives on Mission* (Oxford: Regnum, 1992), ch 5, and George Khodr, 'Christianity in a Pluralistic World – The Economy of the Holy Spirit' in C G Patelos (ed), *The Orthodox Church in the Ecumenical Movement* (Geneva: WCC, 1978), pp 297ff.

20. Mary Clark (ed), *An Aquinas Reader* (London: Hodder & Stoughton, 1972), pp 205f, 257f, 265f.
21. See ARCIC, *Life in Christ: Morals, Communion and the Church* (London: ARCIC, 1994).
22. See further Kevin Ward and Brian Stanley (eds), *The Church Mission Society and World Christianity* (Grand Rapids: Eerdmans, 2000), ch 1, and Bebbington, *Evangelicalism*, pp 71f etc.
23. Leon Howell, *People Are the Subject* (Geneva: WCC, 1980), David Kwang-Sun Suh, *The Korean Minjung in Christ* (Hong Kong: Christian Conference of Asia, 1991), Andrew Kirk, *Liberation Theology: An Evangelical View from the Third World* (London: Marshall, Morgan & Scott, 1979), and the article 'Poor' in Nicholas Lossky *et al.* (eds), *Dictionary of the Ecumenical Movement* (Geneva: WCC, 1991).
24. See, for example, Marshall, *Luke*, pp 249f etc, and Sophie Laws, *The Epistle of James* (London: A & C Black, 1980), pp 102f .
25. There is a huge amount of literature on the subject. For example, Elizabeth Clark, *Women in the Early Church* (Wilmington: Michael Glazier, 1993), Elizabeth and Jürgen Moltmann, *Humanity in God* (London: SCM, 1983), Elisabeth Schüssler Fiorenza, *In Memory of Her: A Feminist Theological Reconstruction of Christian Origins* (London: SCM, 1983), and Elaine Storkey, *What's Right with Feminism* (London: SPCK, 1988).
26. For a summary of these arguments see the correspondence between Robert Runcie, when he was Archbishop of Canterbury, Pope John Paul II and Cardinal Willebrands, *Women Priests: Obstacles to Unity?* (London: CTS, 1986).

27. Thomas FitzGerald and Peter Bouteneff (eds), *Orthodox Reflections on the Way to Harare* (Geneva: WCC, 1998), p 83, italics mine.
28. For a detailed discussion of the notion of 'reception' in the context of the ordination of women see the Eames Commission Report, *Women in the Anglican Episcopate* (Toronto: Anglican Book Centre, 1998), pp 85ff.
29. See further his *Apologia Pro Vita Sua* (London: Collins Fontana, 1959), pp 246ff.

Chapter 3

1. See F F Bruce, *Romans: An Introduction and Commentary* (London: Tyndale, 1963), pp 270f.
2. See further Robert Sider, *The Gospel and Its Proclamation: Message of the Fathers of the Church* (Wilmington: Michael Glazier, 1983), pp 17ff, and John Stambaugh and David Balch, *The Social World of the First Christians* (London: SPCK, 1994), pp 52ff.
3. Lactantius, *The Ante-Nicene Fathers* (Peabody: Hendrickson, 1994), vol 7, p 315, Henry Chadwick, *The Early Church* (Harmondsworth: Penguin, 1967), pp 54f, and a report of the Inter-Faith Consultative Group, *Communities and Buildings* (London: CHP, 1996), pp 32ff.
4. See Justin's *First Apology* in Edward Hardy's *Early Christian Fathers* (Philadelphia: 1953), and Ignatius' *Epistle to the Ephesians* (London: SPCK, 1954), 20:2.
5. Stambaugh and Balch, *The Social World,* p 54.
6. Regarding contacts between these churches see Charles Bigg, *The Epistles of St Peter and St Jude* (Edinburgh: T and T Clark, 1987), pp 67f, and Colin Hemer, *The Letters to the*

Seven Churches of Asia in Their Local Setting (Sheffield: Journal for the Study of the New Testament, 1986), pp 14f.

7. Joseph Lienhard, SJ, *Ministry: Message of the Fathers of the Church* (Wilmington: Michael Glazier, 1984), pp 128ff, and Robert Eno, *Teaching Authority in the Early Church* (Wilmington: Michael Glazier, 1984), pp 84ff.
8. Ignatius, Ephesians 3:2, Irenaeus, *Against the Heresies* in *The Ante-Nicene Fathers*, vol 1, pp 33ff, and Sider, *The Gospel and Its Proclamation*, p 84.
9. See my *From Everywhere to Everywhere* (London: Collins, 1990), pp 40ff. See also Kevin Ward and Brian Stanley (eds), *The Church Mission Society and World Christianity* (Grand Rapids: Eerdmans, 2000), pp 120ff.
10. See, for example, *The Code of Practice* relating to the Church of England's Ecumenical Canons (London: CHP, 1989), pp 24f.

Chapter 4

1. See further John Robinson, *The Body: A Study in Pauline Theology* (London: SCM, 1952), pp 55ff.
2. For further discussion of models of the church in Roman Catholic theology see Avery Dulles's classic *Models of the Church* (Dublin: Gill and Macmillan, 2nd edition, 1987).
3. See, for example, *Working as One Body*, a Report of the Archbishops' Commission on the Organisation of the Church of England (London: CHP, 1995).
4. Pope Pius XII, *Mystici Corporis* (New York: America Press, 1957), 21–3.

5. 'Decree on the Apostolate of the Laity' in Austin Flannery (ed), *Documents of Vatican II*, vol 1 (New York: Costello, 1988), pp 766ff.
6. ARCIC, *Final Report* (London: CTS/SPCK, 1982), p 36.
7. See F F Bruce, *I and II Corinthians* (Grand Rapids: Eerdmans, 1971), p 194.
8. *Baptism, Eucharist and Ministry*, (BEM) Faith and Order Paper, No 111 (Geneva: WCC, 1982), pp 2f, and the *Directory Concerning Ecumenical Matters*, Part I, Flannery, *Documents of Vatican II*, pp 487f.
9. At the Canonisation of the Forty Martyrs of England and Wales, 25 October 1970.
10. See, for example, the Report of the Anglican–Methodist International Commission, *Sharing in the Apostolic Communion* (ACC/WMC, 1996), pp 16f.
11. J Zizioulas, *Being as Communion* (London: DLT, 1985).
12. See the Porvoo Communion Statement with Essays on Church and Ministry in Northern Europe, *Together in Mission and Ministry* (London: CHP, 1993).
13. For example, John Paul II, *Ut Unum Sint* (May They All Be One) (Rome: Vatican, 1995), paras 11f.
14. Lumen Gentium, Flannery, *Documents of Vatican II*, pp 350ff.
15. L Newbigin, *The Gospel in a Pluralist Society* (London: SPCK, 1989), pp 222ff.
16. See Church of England Report, *Good News People: Recognising Diocesan Evangelists* (London: CHP, 1999).
17. See Justin, *First Apology* in *Early Christian Fathers* (trans. E R Hardy) (Philadelphia: 1953), 65–7, and Donald Winslow, 'Gregory Nazianzus and Love for the Poor',

Anglican Theological Review, vol 47, No 4 (October 1965), pp 348ff.

18. John Collins, *Diakonia: Reinterpreting the Ancient Sources* (Oxford: OUP, 1990).
19. Irenaeus, *Against Heresies* 3, 24, 1 (in *Migne's Patrologia Graeca* 7, 966).

Chapter 5

1. On these questions see the Inter-Faith Consultative Group's *Communities and Buildings* (London: CHP, 1996).
2. In the British context such an approach can be seen in the work of the *New Way of Being Church* network. See Peter Price, *Interactive Learning for Churches Building Small Christian Communities* (Sudbury: New Way, 1998).
3. Leonardo Boff, *Ecclesiogenesis* (London: Collins, 1986).
4. Carlos Mesters, *God, Where Are You? Rediscovering the Bible* (New York: Orbis, 1995).
5. Norberto Saracco, 'The Liberating Options of Jesus' in Vinay Samuel and Christopher Sugden (eds), *Sharing Jesus in the Two-Thirds World* (Bangalore: PIM, 1983), pp 49ff.
6. See further Boff, *Ecclesiogenesis*, pp 61ff.
7. Tom O'Loughlin, 'Eucharist or Communion Service', *The Way*, vol 38, pp 365–74.
8. Price, *Interactive Learning*, p 25.
9. Michael Green, *Asian Tigers for Christ: The Dynamic Growth of the Church in S E Asia* (London: SPCK, 2001), pp 43ff.
10. Price, *Interactive Learning*, p 14.
11. S Sykes, 'An Anglican Theology of Evangelism',

Theology, vol XCIIV, no 762 (November/December 1991), pp 405ff.

12. Lesslie Newbigin, *The Gospel in a Pluralist Society* (London: SPCK, 1989), pp 222ff.
13. For Robert Warren's work see *Being Human, Being Church: Spirituality and Mission in the Local Church* (London: HarperCollins, 1995), and *Building Missionary Congregations* (London: CHP, 1995).
14. Raymond Fung, *The Isaiah Vision: An Ecumenical Strategy for Congregational Evangelism* (Geneva: WCC, 1992), p 2.
15. Ann Morisy, *Beyond the Good Samaritan: Community Ministry and Mission* (London: Mowbray, 1997), especially ch 4.
16. *Breaking New Ground* (London: CHP, 1994), especially pp 39f.
17. Susan Billington Harper, *In the Shadow of the Mahatma: Bishop V S Azariah and the Travails of Christianity in British India* (Richmond, Surrey: Curzon, 2000), p 148.
18. See further Stephen Neill, *A History of Christian Missions* (London: Penguin, 1990), pp 139f and 186f.
19. *The Homogeneous Unit Principle* (Wheaton: Lausanne Committee, 1978), David Fraser (ed), *The Church in New Frontiers for Missions* (Monrovia: MARC, 1983), and Edward Dayton and Samuel Wilson (eds), *The Future of World Evangelisation: Unreached Peoples '84* (Monrovia: MARC, 1984).
20. Michael Moynagh and Richard Worsley, *Tomorrow: Using the Future to Understand the Present* (King's Lynn: Lexicon, 2000), pp 105ff.
21. Warren, *Being Human, Being Church*, pp 21ff.

Chapter 6

1. See, for example, Robert Sider, *The Gospel and Its Proclamation: Message of the Fathers of the Church* (Wilmington: Michael Glazier, 1983).
2. Steven Croft, *Ministry in Three Dimensions: Ordination and Leadership in the Local Church* (London: DLT, 1999), pp 38f, and Gordon Kuhrt, *An Introduction to Christian Ministry* (London: CHP, 2000), pp 30f.
3. Church of England Report, *Working as One Body* (London: CHP, 1995), pp 4f.
4. Francis Foulkes, *Ephesians* (Grand Rapids: Eerdmans, 1983), p 117.
5. Croft, *Ministry in Three Dimensions*, pp 85ff.
6. Kuhrt, *An Introduction*, p 28.
7. C Gore, *The Ministry of the Christian Church* (London: Rivington, 1889), pp 394f.
8. Ignatius, *Epistle to the Trallians*, 3, and to the *Ephesians*, 3 (London: SPCK, 1954).
9. Gore, *The Ministry*, pp 271ff, J B Lightfoot, *Epistle to the Philippians* (London: CUP, 1873), pp 189ff.
10. *Stranger in the Wings* (London: CHP, 1998), pp 65f.
11. John Drane, *Cultural Change and Biblical Faith* (Carlisle: Paternoster, 2000), pp 126f.
12. Kuhrt, *An Introduction*, p 9.
13. Tom Wright, *Jesus and the Victory of God* (London: SPCK, 1996), pp 554f.
14. See further Michael Green, *Freed to Serve* (London: Hodder & Stoughton, 1983), 1996, pp 84ff.
15. See further Joseph Lienhard, SJ, *Ministry: Message of the Fathers of the Church* (Wilmington: Michael Glazier, 1984).

16. See, for example, Claus Westermann, *Isaiah 40–66* (London: SCM, 1969), p 423.
17. F F Bruce, *Romans: An Introduction and Commentary* (London: Tyndale, 1971), p 260, C H Dodd, *The Epistle of Paul to the Romans* (London: Fontana, 1959), pp 230f, and Vincent Taylor, *The Epistle to the Romans* (London: Epworth, 1955), pp 93f.
18. See John Robinson, *Wrestling with Romans* (London: SCM, 1979), pp 145f.
19. See 'Church Government X' in David Bercot (ed), *A Dictionary of Early Christian Beliefs* (Peabody: Hendrikson), p 162.
20. Dodd, *The Epistle of Paul to the Romans*, p 231.
21. See further F F Bruce, *I and II Corinthians* (Grand Rapids: Eerdmans, 1971), pp 135f, and John Stott, *Issues Facing Christians Today* (Basingstoke: Marshalls, 1984), pp 251ff.
22. Charles Moule, *The Epistles to the Colossians and to Philemon* (Cambridge: CUP, 1957), p 127.
23. Stott, *Issues*, p 252.
24. Raymond Brown, *An Introduction to the New Testament* (New York: Doubleday, 1996), pp 660f.
25. *Epist ad Cledonium*, Migne's *Patrologia Graeca*, 37, 181C.
26. The correspondence is most conveniently to be found in A Second Report by the House of Bishops, *The Ordination of Women to the Priesthood* (London: CHP, 1988), pp 125ff.
27. See further Gerhard Von Rad, *Genesis* (London: SCM, 1972), pp 57ff.
28. See further Tina Beattie, 'Mary, the Virgin Priest?', *The Month* (December 1996), pp 485ff.

29. In its report on the role of women in the Bible. See Caroll Stuhlmueller cp (ed), *Women and Priesthood: Future Directions* (Minnesota: Liturgical Press, 1978), p 231.
30. Elisabeth Schüssler Fiorenza, *In Memory of Her: A Feminist Theological Reconstruction of Christian Origins* (London: SCM, 1983), pp 172f.
31. Gore, *The Ministry*, p 396.
32. R Runcie, Pope John Paul II and Cardinal Willebrands, *Women Priests: Obstacles to Unity?* (London: CTS, 1986), p 131.
33. See Thomas Fitzgerald and Peter Bouteneff (eds), *Orthodox Reflections on the Way to Harare* (Geneva: WCC, 1998), pp 79ff, and *The Place of the Woman in the Orthodox Church* (Rhodes, 1988).
34. Stuhlmueller, *Women and Priesthood*, pp 60ff, and Beattie, 'Mary', pp 490f.
35. Report of the Archbishops' Group on the Episcopate, *Episcopal Ministry* (the 'Cameron Report') (London: CHP, 1990), pp 310f.
36. John Stambaugh and David Balch, *The Social World of the First Christians* (London: SPCK, 1994), p 55.
37. Peter Phan, *Social Thought: Message of the Fathers of the Church* (Wilmington: Michael Glazier, 1984), pp 37f.
38. See further Lienhard, *Ministry*, pp 37, 42, 132, etc.
39. David Sceats, 'Orders and Officers of the Church' in Ian Bunting (ed), *Celebrating the Anglican Way* (London: Hodder & Stoughton, 1996), p 197, and Nigel Scotland, *Good and Proper Men: Lord Palmerston and the Bench of Bishops* (Cambridge: James Clarke, 2000), p 72.

Chapter 7

1. See further Susan Billington Harper, *In the Shadow of the Mahatma: Bishop V S Azariah and the Travails of Christianity in British India* (Richmond, Surrey: Curzon, 2000), pp 147f, 307ff.
2. *Lumen Gentium* 8, *Unitatis Redintegratio* 3ff in Austin Flannery op (ed), *Documents of Vatican II*, vol 1 (New York: Costello, 1988), pp 357f and 455f.
3. See further Michael Nazir-Ali, 'The Gift of Authority: A United, Reformed and Renewed Church?', *Anvil*, vol 17, no 4 (2000), pp 300f. See also *One Bread One Body*, a teaching document on the Eucharist of the Catholic Bishops' Conferences of England, Wales, Ireland and Scotland (London: Catholic Truth Society, 1998), and the response to it by the House of Bishops of the Church of England, *The Eucharist: Sacrament of Unity* (London: CHP, 2001).
4. For a discussion of some of these issues see the *Assembly Workbook* of the WCC's Harare Assembly, Geneva, 1998, and Michael Nazir-Ali, 'So that the World May Believe', in *One in Christ* 1996–2, pp 99ff.
5. See, for example, Colin Buchanan, Eric Mascall, Jim Packer and Graham Leonard, *Growing into Union: Proposals for Forming a United Church in England* (London: SPCK, 1970), pp 130ff.
6. Report of the Episcopal–Lutheran Drafting Team, *Called to Common Mission*, 1998.
7. W J Marshall, *Faith and Order in the North India–Pakistan Plan: A Theological Assessment* (London: Friends of CNI, 1978), especially ch 3.
8. *Ministry in a Uniting Church: From Recognition to*

Reconciliation (Swansea: Commission of Covenanted Churches, 1986).

9. See further *The Porvoo Common Statement* (London: CHP, 1993), and *Together in Mission and Ministry* (London: CHP, 1993).
10. *Called to Be One* (London: CTE, 1996), p 27.
11. Michael Nazir-Ali, *Mission and Dialogue: Proclaiming the Gospel Afresh in Every Age* (London: SPCK, 1995), pp 50f.
12. K Raiser, *Ecumenism in Transition: A Paradigm Shift in the Ecumenical Movement* (Geneva: WCC, 1991).
13. Claudius Ceccon and Kristian Paludan, *My Neighbour – Myself: Visions of Diakonia* (Geneva: WCC, 1988).

Chapter 8

1. Robert Sider, *The Gospel and Its Proclamation: Message of the Fathers of the Church* (Wilmington: Michael Glazier, 1983), pp 60ff.
2. Charles Bigg, *The Epistles of St. Peter and St. Jude* (Edinburgh: T and T Clark, 1987), pp 24ff, and Henry Bettenson (ed), *Documents of the Christian Church* (Oxford: OUP, 1974), pp 7ff.
3. See William Young, *Patriarch, Shah and Caliph* (Rawalpindi: Christian Study Centre, 1974), pp 27f.
4. Jaroslav Pelikan, *The Excellent Empire: The Fall of Rome and the Triumph of the Church* (San Francisco: Harper and Row, 1987), especially ch 6.
5. Paul Welsby, *How the Church of England Works* (London: CIO, 1985), pp 4, 48f.
6. Michael Nazir-Ali and Colin Podmore in *Working with*

the Spirit: Choosing Diocesan Bishops (London: CHP, 2001), pp 103ff.

7. Nigel Scotland, *Good and Proper Men: Lord Palmerston and the Bench of Bishops* (Cambridge: James Clarke, 2000), pp 7f, 28ff, 158ff.
8. See further Michael Nazir-Ali, 'A Spiritual and Moral Framework for Society' in Tariq Modood (ed), *Church, State and Religious Minorities* (London: Policy Studies Institute, 1997), pp 31ff.
9. Michael Nazir-Ali, *Mission and Dialogue: Proclaiming the Gospel Afresh in Every Age* (London: SPCK, 1995), p 57.
10. Modood, *Church*, pp 3ff, John Habgood, *Finding a Moral Heart for Europe* (Windsor: St George's House, 1992), James Beckford and Sophie Gilliat, *The Church of England and Other Faiths in a Multi-Faith Society* (Coventry: University of Warwick, 1996).
11. David Nicholls, 'Addressing God as Ruler', *British Journal of Sociology*, vol 44 (March 1993).
12. Owen Chadwick, *The Reformation* (London: Penguin, 1990), pp 97ff, E A Benians, *John Fisher* (Cambridge: CUP, 1935), and R M and A J Carlyle, *Hugh Latimer* (London: Methuen, 1899).
13. See further Michael Nazir-Ali, *From Everywhere to Everywhere* (London: Collins, 1990), pp 51f, J Dowden, *The Scottish Communion Office 1764* (Oxford: OUP, 1922), and Colin Buchanan, 'Anglican Liturgy' in *A New Dictionary of Liturgy and Worship* (London: SCM, 1986), pp 322–5.
14. David Nicholls and Rowan Williams, *Politics and Theological Identity* (London: Jubilee, 1984), and John

D Davies, *The Faith Abroad* (Oxford: Blackwell, 1983), pp 42ff.

15. See further the Report of the Archbishop of Canterbury's Commission on Urban Priority Areas, *Faith in the City* (London: CHP, 1985), and the sequel, *Staying in the City* (London: CHP, 1995).
16. For examples of the church's work in these areas see the House of Bishops teaching document *Marriage* (London: CHP, 1999), the Report of a Working Party on Human Fertilisation and Embryology of the Board for Social Responsibility, *Personal Origins* (London: CHP, 2nd revised edn, 1996). See also the Church of Scotland's *Preconceived Ideas: A Christian Perspective on IVF and Embryology* (Edinburgh: St Andrew's Press, 1996), the Joint Submission on Euthanasia from the Church of England's House of Bishops and the Roman Catholic Bishops Conference of England and Wales to the House of Lords Select Committee on Medical Ethics, July 1993, and *On Dying Well*, a contribution to the euthanasia debate (London: CHP, 2nd edn, 2000.
17. Royal Commission on the Reform of the House of Lords, *A House for the Future* (London: The Stationery Office, 2000), pp 150ff.
18. Walter Brueggemann, *Hopeful Imagination: Prophetic Voices in Exile* (Philadelphia: Fortress, 1986), pp 90ff etc.
19. A MacIntyre, *After Virtue* (London: Duckworth, 2000), pp 204.
20. D Hope, 'Changing Church: Unchanging God', Cambridge, 4th February 2001.
21. See further Michael Nazir-Ali, *Frontiers in Muslim–Christian Encounter* (Oxford: Regnum, 1987), *The Roots of*

Islamic Tolerance: Origin and Development, Oxford Project for Peace Studies, no 26 (1990), and 'Law and Religion' in *Islam and Christian–Muslim Relations*, vol 11, no 2 (July 2000).

22. *United States Policies in Support of Religious Freedom: Focus on Christians*, 22nd July 1997.

And Finally . . .

1. *The Apostolic Fathers*, vol 2 (Cambridge, MA: Harvard University Press, 1992), pp 359f.

A Study Guide for Groups

1. C F C Masterman, *The Condition of England*, 1909, quoted in David L Edwards, *Christian England*, vol 3 (London: Fount, 1989), p 346.
2. Quoted in *ibid.*, p 346.
3. *Ibid.*, p 350.
4. *Ibid.*, p 361.
5. Mick Brown, *The Spiritual Tourist*, quoted in David Lewis and Darren Bridger, *The Soul of the New Consumer* (London: Nicholas Brealey, 2001).

For Further Reading

Alison, James, *Knowing Jesus* (London: SPCK, 1993)

Anglican–Methodist International Commission, *Sharing in the Apostolic Communion* (ACC/WMC, 1996)

ARCIC, *Life in Christ: Morals, Communion and the Church* (London: ARCIC, 1994)

ARCIC, *The Gift of Authority* (Toronto and London: Anglican Book Centre/CTS, 1999)

Aulen, Gustav, *Christus Victor* (London: SPCK, 1950)

Batey, Richard A, *Jesus and the Forgotten City* (Grand Rapids: Eerdmans, 1991)

Bebbington, David, *Evangelicalism in Modern Britain* (London: Unwin Hyman, 1989)

Beckford, James, and Sophie Gilliat, *The Church of England and Other Faiths in a Multi-Faith Society* (Coventry: University of Warwick, 1996)

Billington Harper, Susan, *In the Shadow of the Mahatma: Bishop V S Azariah and the Travails of Christianity in British India* (Richmond, Surrey: Curzon, 2000)

Boff, Leonardo, *Ecclesiogenesis* (London: Collins, 1986)

Brown, David, *Tradition and Imagination: Revelation and Change* (Oxford: OUP, 1999)

Brown, Raymond, *An Introduction to the New Testament* (New York: Doubleday, 1996)

Brueggemann, William, *Hopeful Imagination: Prophetic Voices in Exile* (Philadelphia: Fortress, 1986)

Buchanan, Colin, Eric Mascall, Jim Packer and Graham Leonard, *Growing into Union: Proposals for Forming a United Church in England* (London: SPCK, 1970)

Bunting, Ian (ed), *Celebrating the Anglican Way* (London: Hodder & Stoughton, 1996)

Carlyle, R M and A J, *Hugh Latimer* (London: Methuen, 1899)

Ceccon, Claudius, and Kristian Paludan, *My Neighbour – Myself: Visions of Diakonia* (Geneva: WCC, 1988)

Chadwick, Henry, *The Early Church* (Harmondsworth: Penguin, 1967)

Chadwick, Owen, *The Reformation* (London: Penguin, 1990)

Church of England Report, *The Search for Faith and the Witness of the Church* (London: CHP, 1996)

Church of England Report, *Good News People: Recognising Diocesan Evangelists* (London: CHP, 1999)

Church of England Report of a Working Party on Human Fertilisation and Embryology of the Board of Social Responsibility, *Personal Origins* (London: CHP, 1996)

Church of England Report of the Archbishop of Canterbury's Commission on Urban Priority Areas, *Faith in the City* (London: CHP, 1985), and sequel, *Staying in the City* (London: CHP, 1995)

Church of England Report of the Archbishops' Commission

on the Organisation of the Church of England, *Working as One Body* (London: CHP, 1995)

Church of England report on Ordained Local Ministry, *Stranger in the Wings* (London: CHP, 1998)

Church of England Report on Church Planting, *Breaking New Ground* (London: CHP, 1994)

Churches in Wales Report, *Ministry in a Uniting Church: From Recognition to Reconciliation* (Swansea: Commission of the Covenanted Churches, 1986)

Clark, Elizabeth, *Women in the Early Church* (Wilmington: Michael Glazier, 1993)

Clark, Mary (ed), *An Aquinas Reader* (London: Hodder & Stoughton, 1972)

Coles, Robert, *The Spiritual Life of Children* (Boston: Mifflin, 1990)

Collins, John, *Diakonia: Reinterpreting the Ancient Sources* (Oxford: OUP, 1990)

Croft, Steven, *Ministry in Three Dimensions: Ordination and Leadership in the Local Church* (London: DLT, 1999)

Davie, Grace, *Religion in Britain since 1945: Believing without Belonging* (Oxford: Blackwell, 1994)

Davies, John D, *The Faith Abroad* (Oxford: Blackwell, 1983)

Davies, Paul, *The Mind of God* (London: Penguin, 1992)

Dayton, Edward, and Samuel Wilson (eds), *The Future of World Evangelisation: Unreached Peoples '84* (Monrovia: MARC, 1984)

Drane, John, *Cultural Change and Biblical Faith* (Carlisle: Paternoster, 2000)

Dulles, Avery, *Models of the Church* (Dublin: Gill and Macmillan, 2nd edition 1987)

Dunn, James, *Unity and Diversity in the New Testament* (London: SCM, 1990)

Eames Commission Report, *Women in the Anglican Episcopate* (Toronto: Anglican Book Centre, 1998)

Eliot, T S, *Four Quartets* (London: Faber, 1970)

Eno, Robert, *Teaching Authority in the Early Church* (Wilmington: Michael Glazier, 1984)

Finaldi, Gabriele, *The Image of Christ* (London: National Gallery, 2000)

Fiorenza, Elisabeth Schüssler, *In Memory of Her: A Feminist Theological Reconstruction of Christian Origins* (London: SCM, 1983)

FitzGerald, Thomas, and Peter Bouteneff (eds), *Orthodox Reflections on the Way to Harare* (Geneva: WCC, 1998)

Flannery, Austin (ed), *Decree on the Apostolate of the Laity*, Documents of Vatican II, vol 1 (New York: Costello, 1988)

Fraser, David (ed), *The Church in New Frontiers for Missions* (Monrovia: MARC, 1983)

Fung, Raymond, *The Isaiah Vision: An Ecumenical Strategy for Congregational Evangelism* (Geneva: WCC, 1992)

Gill, Robin, *The Myth of the Empty Church* (London: SPCK, 1993)

Gore, Charles, *The Ministry of the Christian Church* (London: Rivington, 1889)

Government Report on the Royal Commission on the Reform of the House of Lords, *A House for the Future* (London: The Stationery Office, 2000)

Green, Anthony, RA, *Resurrection: A Pictorial Sculpture for the Millennium* (London: Napier Jones, 1999)

Green, Michael, *Asian Tigers for Christ: The Dynamic Growth of the Church in S E Asia* (London: SPCK, 2001)

Green, Michael, *Freed to Serve* (London: Hodder & Stoughton, 1983)

Habgood, John, *Finding a Moral Heart for Europe* (Windsor: St George's House, 1992)

Hay, David, and Kate Hunt, *Understanding the Spirituality of People Who Don't Go to Church* (Centre for the Study of Human Relations, University of Nottingham final report, August 2000)

Hay, David, and Rebecca Nye, *The Spirit of the Child* (London: HarperCollins, 1998)

Hemer, Colin, *The Letters to the Seven Churches of Asia in Their Local Setting* (Sheffield: Journal for the Study of the New Testament, 1986)

Herbert, George, *The Works of George Herbert* (Ware: Wordsworth Library, 1994)

Hill, Henry (ed), *Light from the East* (Toronto: Anglican Book Centre, 1988)

House of Bishops, a Second Report, *The Ordination of Women to the Priesthood* (London: CHP, 1988)

House of Bishops of the Church of England, *The Eucharist: Sacrament of Unity* (London: CHP, 2001)

House of Bishops teaching document, *Marriage* (London: CHP, 1999)

Howell, Leon, *People Are the Subject* (Geneva: WCC, 1980)

Inter-Faith Consultative Group report, *Communities and Buildings* (London: CHP, 1996)

John Paul II, *Ut Unum Sint (May They All Be One)* (Rome: Vatican, 1995)

Keshishian, Aram, *Orthodox Perspectives on Mission* (Oxford: Regnum, 1992)

Kirk, Andrew, *Liberation Theology: An Evangelical View from the Third World* (London: Marshall, Morgan & Scott, 1979)

Kuhrt, Gordon, *An Introduction to Christian Ministry* (London: CHP, 2000)

Kwang-Sun Suh, David, *The Korean Minjung in Christ* (Hong Kong: Christian Conference of Asia, 1991)

Lienhard, Joseph, S J, *Ministry: Message of the Fathers of the Church* (Wilmington: Michael Glazier, 1984)

Lossky, Nicholas, *et al.* (eds), *Dictionary of the Ecumenical Movement* (Geneva: WCC, 1991)

Lovelock, J, *Gaia: A New Look at Life on Earth* (Oxford: OUP, 1979)

MacGavran, Donald, *The Homogeneous Unit Principle* (Wheaton: Lausanne Committee, 1978)

MacIntyre, Alasdair, *After Virtue* (London: Duckworth, 2000)

Marshall, W J, *Faith and Order in the North India–Pakistan Plan: A Theological Assessment* (London: Friends of CNI, 1978)

Mesters, Carlos, *God, Where Are You? Rediscovering the Bible* (New York: Orbis, 1995)

Modood, Tariq (ed), *Church, State and Religious Minorities* (London: Policy Studies Institute, 1997)

Moltmann, Jürgen and Elizabeth, *Humanity in God* (London: SCM, 1983)

Montefiore, Hugh, *The Probability of God* (London: SCM, 1985)

Morisy, Ann, *Beyond the Good Samaritan: Community Ministry and Mission* (London: Mowbray, 1997)

Moule, Charles, *The Birth of the New Testament* (London: A & C Black, 1962)

Moynagh, Michael, and Richard Worsley, *Tomorrow: Using the Future to Understand the Present* (Kings Lynn: Lexicon, 2000)

Nazir-Ali, Michael, *Citizens and Exiles: Christian Faith in a Plural World* (London: SPCK, 1998)

Nazir-Ali, Michael, *From Everywhere to Everywhere* (London: Collins, 1990)

Nazir-Ali, Michael, *Frontiers in Muslim–Christian Encounter* (Oxford: Regnum, 1987)

Nazir-Ali, Michael, *Islam: A Christian Perspective* (Exeter: Paternoster, 1983)

Nazir-Ali, Michael, *Mission and Dialogue: Proclaiming the Gospel Afresh in Every Age* (London: SPCK, 1995)

Nazir-Ali, Michael, *The Roots of Islamic Tolerance: Origin and Development*, Oxford Project for Peace Studies, no 26 (1990)

Neill, Stephen, *A History of Christian Missions* (London: Penguin, 1990)

Newbigin, Lesslie, *The Gospel in a Pluralist Society* (London: SPCK, 1989)

Newman, John Henry, *Apologia Pro Vita Sua* (London: Collins Fontana, 1959)

Nicholls, David, 'Addressing God as Ruler', *British Journal of Sociology*, vol 44 (March 1993)

Nicholls, David, and Rowan Williams, *Politics and Theological Identity* (London: Jubilee, 1984)

Nouwen, Henri, *The Wounded Healer* (New York: Doubleday, 1979)

O'Donovan, Oliver, *Resurrection and the Moral Order* (Leicester: IVP, 1986)

Patelos, C G (ed), *The Orthodox Church in the Ecumenical Movement* (Geneva: WCC, 1978)

Pelikan, Jaroslav, *The Excellent Empire: The Fall of Rome and the Triumph of the Church* (San Francisco: Harper and Row, 1987)

Phan, Peter, *Social Thought: Message of the Fathers of the Church* (Wilmington: Michael Glazier, 1984)

Polkinghorne, John, trilogy, *One World*, *Science and Creation* and *Science and Providence* (London: SPCK, 1986–89)

Porvoo Common Statement with Essays on Church and Ministry in Northern Europe, *Together in Mission and Ministry* (London: CHP, 1993)

Price, Peter, *Interactive Learning for Churches Building Small Christian Communities* (Sudbury: New Way, 1998)

Raiser, Konrad, *Ecumenism in Transition: A Paradigm Shift in the Ecumenical Movement* (Geneva: WCC, 1991)

Reardon, Martin (ed), *Called to Be One* (London: CTE, 1996)

Robinson, John, *The Body: A Study in Pauline Theology* (London: SCM, 1952)

Runcie, Robert, Pope John Paul II and Cardinal Willebrands, *Women Priests: Obstacles to Unity?* (London: CTS, 1986)

Sacks, Oliver, *The Man Who Mistook his Wife for a Hat* (London: Picador, 1986)

Samuel, Vinay, and Christopher Sugden (eds), *Proclaiming Christ in Christ's Way* (Oxford: Regnum, 1989)

Samuel, Vinay, and Christopher Sugden (eds), *Sharing Jesus in the Two-Thirds World* (Bangalore: PIM, 1983)

Sanneh, Lamin, *Translating the Message – The Missionary Impact on Culture* (New York: Orbis, 1989)

Scotland, Nigel, *Good and Proper Men: Lord Palmerston and the Bench of Bishops* (Cambridge: James Clarke, 2000)

Sider, Robert, *The Gospel and Its Proclamation: Message of the Fathers of the Church* (Wilmington: Michael Glazier, 1983)

Stambaugh, John, and David Balch, *The Social World of the First Christians* (London: SPCK, 1994)

Stannard, Russell, *Science and the Renewal of Belief* (London: SCM, 1982)

Storkey, Elaine, *What's Right with Feminism* (London: SPCK, 1988)

Stuhlmueller, Caroll cp (ed), *Women and Priesthood: Future Directions* (Minnesota: Liturgical Press, 1978)

The Catholic Bishops' Conferences of England, Wales, Ireland and Scotland, *One Bread One Body: A Teaching Document on the Eucharist* (London: Catholic Truth Society, 1998)

The Church of Scotland, *Preconceived Ideas: A Christian Perspective on IVF and Embryology* (Edinburgh: St Andrew's Press, 1996)

Ward, Kevin, and Brian Stanley (eds), *The Church Mission Society and World Christianity* (Grand Rapids: Eerdmans, 2000)

Warren, Robert, *Being Human, Being Church: Spirituality and Mission in the Local Church* (London: HarperCollins, 1995)

Warren, Robert, *Building Missionary Congregations* (London: CHP, 1995)

Welsby, Paul, *How the Church of England Works* (London: CIO, 1985)

Wessels, Anton, *Europe: Was It Ever Really Christian?* (London: SCM, 1994)

World Council of Churches Faith and Order Paper, No 111, *Baptism, Eucharist and Ministry* (BEM) (Geneva: WCC, 1982)

Wright, Tom, *Jesus and the Victory of God* (London: SPCK, 1996)

Young, William, *Patriarch, Shah and Caliph* (Rawalpindi: Christian Study Centre, 1974)

Zahl, Paul, *The Protestant Face of Anglicanism* (Grand Rapids: Eerdmans, 1998)

Zizioulas, John, *Being as Communion* (London: DLT, 1985)

Index of Names, Places and Subjects

M

N

Index of Biblical References

Liberated to Lead

by Colin Buckland

This unique book is design to enhance the effectiveness of full-time leaders in Christian ministry or mission. Used prayerfully, the exercises and points for reflection will enable you to:

- balance family life and the pressures of ministry
- cultivate a healthy attitude to power in ministry roles
- settle on realistic expectations in ministry
- gain an introduction to self-awareness skills
- clarify your sense of calling to Christian service
- avoid unnecessary sexual problems
- overcome or prevent burnout

THE REVD COLIN D BUCKLAND has more than 23 years' experience as a pastor, and more than 18 years' as a consultant, trainer and counsellor to church leaders, churches and Christian organisations.

FUTURECHURCH